Larry Warwaruk

To Find Myhailo

Cover Art: Raquel Simonson 2021

Larry Warwaruk
January 26, 1943 - June 29 2017

During his final weeks, as our father rested, he often held this manuscript; adding a note, taking away a word here or there, weaving the story of Myhailo, and of himself.

It was his final wish - to have this book published. "Myhailo" he whispered, the last word he spoke to me.

Now, here it is, in its published form.

For you Dad, I love you.
- Varina

We tried to keep the manuscript for this book as close to the original as possible. Special thank you to Dad's friend Wayne Kallio, who helped with formatting and editing.

Thank you to Natasha Warwaruk and Stephen Warwaruk for proofreading.

To Find Myhailo

CHAPTER 1

The 10th week after Easter, 1945,
They took Myhailo Warwaruk.
I would have been not yet three...
My first consciousness -
a memory
of me standing in my crib.

Seven decades later
I pretend this to be the moment of
Myhailo's death throes
calling from the Carpathian forests.

In the shadows of these devil's hills
lurk the ghosts of Stepan Bandera's insurgents.
From somewhere deep in the forest
Myhailo's ghost watches
as the fight continues.

Larry Warwaruk

Varvar in Ukrainian means *barbarian*... My name is *Warwaruk*, with the *W*, not the *V*. The *W* is Polish. You need to understand that.

My great grandparents, Danylo and Maria, with sons Stepan and Wasyl, and daughter Pazia, emigrated in May of 1903 from a Polish-dominated corner of the Austrian Empire. The bulk of my genetics came from this family. Wasyl was my paternal grandfather. Pazia, my maternal great grandmother, her daughter being my mother's mother.

Uk means *little*. As I dig down to my roots, I ponder this meaning of my Ukrainian name, *Varvaruk;* language wars play no small part in the jigsaw of Ukrainians' eccentricities.

Ivan Franko, Ukrainian writer at the time of Danylo and Maria's emigration, shows some dark traits in his fairytale, *Fox Mykyta*. A decade ago I started on my story *To Find Myhailo,* and as the time passed, the deeper I got into the caverns of my own dark side, I found a heritage coloured bright with art and flowers, yet strangely dark in deed. Fox Mykyta plays a part in the Myhailo story. Through my decade of searching, I began to see the fox as the mouthpiece for a universal proverb:

Only fools and children tell the truth.

My roots are in *Halychyna*. English maps show the region as *Galicia*. Danylo and his family left from there to settle in the woods off the southern shores of Manitoba's Lake Winnipegosis, at what later became known as the Volga District. The surveys had been underway, but because the land was burdened with willow bluffs, poplar stands, swamp grass, rocks, and water, as of 1903, township 30 and the north half of 29 were not as yet completely chained off. But Danylo and his two sons each claimed a quarter section regardless. They could register the homesteads later.

To Find Myhailo

A hundred years have passed, and in Ukraine the Warwaruk home village of Vovkhivsti has become the base for my current search to find Myhailo Warwaruk's story.

In my youth and middle years I had no interest whatsoever in this heritage, no interest in things Ukrainian. When I was three my parents ran a general store they had bought in the mostly English and Scottish Saskatchewan village of Glenavon. It was the place and time for my mother and father to try to hide their Ukrainian accents. When Mother worked in the store, an old Scottish neighbour woman was my babysitter. She didn't try to hide her accent. I faintly remember standing in my crib, scared of her.

Saskatchewan has many third generation descendants of European immigrants. My wife Mavis is one of these descendants, and like so many of our generation, in our senior years, we take a growing interest to explore the lands of our forebears. In the summer of 2007 we visited Finland, and then Ukraine. At that time I knew nothing of Myhailo.

Larry Warwaruk

*A gentle place
like mine when I was three
Green grass and trees and paths
to run and play and dream...*

To Find Myhailo

The wooded foothills of the Carpathian Mountains stretch down to Vovkhivsti. Birds chirp, and I think of a dream. I'm a little boy. Across the alley from our backyard in Glenavon, an empty old wood shed sags, ready to fall apart. In the shed are three graves, and a name is carved on the middle headstone. All at once a brown bird with yellow feet and a broken wing flops down on the graves. A bird with bright blue feathers, beady eyes, and a sharp beak flies in. It scolds the crippled bird, chasing it off the graves and out to the alley.

At a Ukrainian museum in Saskatoon, one week after I had this dream, I came upon a display of Carpathian folklore. The two birds of my dream were perched on an evergreen tree. The brown one, the Kite, is doomed to sing with a painful screech because it wouldn't clean the mud from the bottom of a well. It didn't want to get its beautiful yellow feet dirty. The blue one is the Cuckoo, known in Ukraine as the bird of all knowledge who knows when you are going to die.

These two birds had emerged from my gene pool. They were nothing I had ever seen in my lifetime, and I found out later that the name etched on the headstone was that of the man who translated at the immigration hall in Winnipeg when my ancestors arrived.

They had left the lush beauty of Vovkhivsti, to fight rocks and roots and mire in Manitoba on the shores of Lake Winnipegosis. And here I am now, a century later, a Warwaruk returning to the homeland river valley, a sight that could be photographed for the cover on a book of fairytales.

Larry Warwaruk

*They come
like a parade of pilgrims.
Throngs of beasts
of every kind and shape.
Squeaking, barking.
Howling, quacking.
Singing songs and flying banners.*

To Find Myhailo

Ivan Franko had a German father and a Ukrainian mother. Born and raised in Halychyna, he knew the region's ethnic mix. The animals in his fairytale *Fox Mykyta* can be seen as Russian bears, Polish wolves, Jewish goats; Romanians, Hungarians - all rushing to meet the demands of the Austrian ruler in Lviv. The animals heed to the call of the Lion King. Skirting the pack is Fox Mykyta, the Ukrainian anarchist who refuses to join the parade.

These were the people of Halychyna. There were many Ukrainians, Poles, Romanians, Hungarians, Jews, Gypsies... In the fairytale, Tsar Lion's task was to keep his Realm in order, while the fox's task was simply to survive. Because some of the other animals are more powerful than he is, Mykyta tells them what they want to hear, always part of his scheme to steal a sausage, or save himself from being hanged from a tree. Many of the animals that aren't as powerful, like the chickens, he simply kills and eats.

Fox Mykyta's landscape was the domain of the Warwaruks. Dark and lighter greens of thick hardwood forest reach up from Vovkhivsti to the far horizon of the Carpathians. The sun plays with the clouds to cast mysterious shadows. The light breaks through to paint light patches, and in other places - in the dips and on the hills, dark shadows cover the mysteries. Throughout these hills are isolated dwellings, and small fields and meadows interspersed among the trees. In Ivan Franko's fairytale, Fox Mykyta would hole up in these wooded mountains, just as did Stepan Bandera's nationalist insurgents half a century later.

And another half a century later in the village, I see storks nesting on chimneys and at the top of Soviet built concrete power poles. In the long alley between the rows of houses with their front yards and iron-work gates, a horse drawn rubber-tired wagon overflows with loose hay. A young man holds the reins. I look out to a common pasture where an old man sits on a stool. He's taking his turn to watch his and five of his neighbours' milk cows.

In a mammoth garden beyond her backyard, an old woman bends over in the hot sun, her hoe chopping the weeds that dare to grow. All along the stretch of gardens behind other backyards, more old women and the odd old man swelter in the heat. A grandmother, wearing a babushka and brandishing a willow twig, herds seven goslings.

In one front yard is an ancient open well; its weighted long pole points skyward. The well has the appearance of a long-necked crane. And that is its Ukrainian name, *Jouroval*.

I saw wells like this in 2007.

To Find Myhailo

CHAPTER 2

*The Kite and the
Cuckoo bird had called me
in my dream...
And here I'm called again
on the first return to my roots.*

Inside the terminal at Kyiv's airport, a young woman holds up a sign - *Warwaruk*.

"I am *Sofiya*," she says, and then she hugs us - first me, then Mavis.

"We take taxi to the hotel," she says. "Forty-five *hrynia*. You can exchange money here, or use the ATM when we get into the city. One American dollar for five hrynia."

We check in at our hotel, then walk to the metro which takes us to the centre of the city. My first impressions are of Lexus and Mercedes cars, beautiful women wearing spiked heels, and the golden arches of MacDonalds high up on the face of a Soviet-era building.

At the centre of a large square, a towering obelisk honours the 1991 Independence of Ukraine. Across from the square are the Parliament Building and the President's Palace.

In this square during the 2004 Orange Revolution, Sofiya had inserted flowers into the rifle barrels of Kyiv's militia. Flowers play a role in Ukraine's politics.

Here was the start of *Maidan,* the first ousting of the pro-Russian Viktor Yanukovych. In November, he had been elected President, but his pro-western rival, Viktor Yushchenko, contested the results. Thousands came from the west - from Lviv and area to protest. They camped for two months in Independence Square until Yanukovych relented and called a new election which Viktor Yushchenko won. Like many educated young Ukrainians, for the first time in her life, Sofiya felt that the Ukrainian people could actually do something to bring about change.

Sofiya is an English Language major from the university in Lviv. For two days here in Kyiv she'll be our guide. She will then send Mavis and me on a night train west to Lviv where two of her classmates are to meet us. Olya and

To Find Myhailo

Natalya will be the ones to help us find the Warwaruk village, but first things first. Sofiya will show us the sites of Kyiv, the capital of Ukraine.

She points out the obelisk - a maiden holding high a banner that spells *Ukraine*. Sofiya takes a picture of Mavis and me standing outside the doorway of the President's Palace. She shows us St. Sophia, Kyiv's ancient church claimed by three Orthodox patriarchies: that of Moscow, Kyiv, and the Autocephalous.

Centuries ago, Kyiv was the home of the Orthodox Church. But then the Tartar invasions forced its Patriarch and many of the landlords to flee to the forested northeast. Over time these Ukrainians inter-mingled with the Finno-Urgic population. A new Russian identity formed, and the Moscow Patriarchy took root. Following the Russian Revolution, a Kyiv-centred Orthodoxy split away from Moscow's control. Two new groups formed - the Ukrainian Orthodox Church - Kyiv Patriarchy, and the Autocephalous Patriarchy, each claiming ownership of St. Sophia. Even the Ukrainian Catholic Church that's centred in Lviv makes a claim for St. Sophia. Most of the bishops and priests in the Ukrainian orthodox Church, Moscow Patriarchy, are Ukrainian, yet nearly all of them speak Russian.

Our young guide takes us to more church buildings - to the *Lavra* that overlooks the high banks of the Dnieper River. At the entry to these grounds the ruins of a bombed out church are covered with a plexiglass dome.

"The Russians blamed the Germans," Sofiya says, "but really it was the Soviets who did it." Beside this display of the ruins stands a towering new church.

"An exact replica," Sofiya says, "Built after we got independence. All the paintings done exactly as they were."

The Dnieper riverbank displays gigantic opposites. Beyond acres of churches are more acres of military tanks and guns, and huge figures of Red Army heroes crafted in the style of Soviet Realism.

In a few years on this hillside will be built the museum to show the deep sorrow of *Holodomor - The Hunger* - the Soviet starvation of millions of Ukrainians in 1932/33. At the front of the building will stand a statue of an emaciated child. She will hold a single head of wheat. If Stalin had caught her picking it up from the stubble... The message is clear. This will be the eternal memory of Holodomor!

In my home province of Saskatchewan, the Ukrainian Canadian Congress will fund a duplication of the little girl statue to stand on the grounds of the provincial legislature.

"Underneath the riverbank," Sofiya says. "Caves where hermits lived. Their bodies are still there from a thousand years. We'll see them."

"Do you know what century the hermits no longer came to live in these caves?"

"I don't know," Sofiya says. "But I will ask."

A monk, with a grey beard down to his chest, stands in the courtyard. The folds of his black robe fall to his sandals. He talks on a cell phone. Sofiya approaches him when he's done with his phone conversation. When she asks, he snaps at her, pauses, and then his voice softens.

"What was that all about?" I ask her.

"He said I should speak Russian, not Ukrainian."

"What did he say about the hermits?"

"He said they quit coming to the Lavra in the 16th century when they lost the Holy Spirit."

The caves are dark and narrow, the hermit cells carved into the earthen walls. Each cell has a glass-covered

To Find Myhailo

coffin with the mummified remains of a hermit. People walk single-file, some carrying lit candles. Mavis wears my hat because in the churches of the Moscow Patriarchy, women must cover their heads. Most of the people in this dark walkway through the caves are worshipers - most of them old women who pray at each cell. They make the sign of the cross three times, kiss a glass-covered coffin, make the sign of the cross three times again, and continue on to the next cell. Here and there, a bearded monk stands guard.

Sofiya then puts us on a boat to see the sights from the river's shore. Halfway up the riverbank hovers the cross-holding statue of St. Volodomyr, the founder of Kyiv. All along the upper bank are the domes of the Lavra churches. To the south, a Soviet statue of Mother Ukraine - The Motherland - holds a sword pointed high to the sky, its tip higher than the church crosses on the Lavra skyline.

"But look," Sofiya says. "To the north." The Church of St. Andrew stands on Kyiv's highest hill. The cross mounted on the church's uppermost dome is higher than the Soviet sword. Sofiya doesn't tell us that the sword had its tip snipped off when Ukraine got its independence in 1991.

In the evening she takes us to the train station. I hand her money to buy our tickets for our night train to Lviv.

The train reminds me of rides I took as a child, when my parents sent me on the train for dentist appointments in Regina. Our car to Lviv has a toilet at one end - the old-fashioned kind that dumps the waste outside. I can remember from my childhood rides, looking down through the toilet hole as railway ties passed swiftly underneath. We have an enclosed sleeper compartment with two double bunks, all to ourselves. A woman attendant hands us clean blankets, and in the very early morning serves us tea.

It's 6:30 a.m. when our train screeches to a stop in the Lviv rail yards. A young woman stands on the platform beside an older man holding onto a bicycle. We step down from the railcar as she studies us, then nods to the man beside her. He nods back and leaves with his bicycle.

"I'm Olya!"

A moment later another young woman appears: "I'm Natalya." The two could well be sisters, and hardly out of their teens. Natalya tells us that our hotel room won't be ready until the afternoon, so we can go to her boyfriend's apartment to shower and have a bite to eat. And maybe have a rest after our long train ride.

The Soviet-era apartment block has light bulbs missing in its dark and unpainted hallway. The tiny elevator shakes and creaks all the way to the 7th floor that has another dark hallway. Natalya pulls out a ring of six keys from her purse. The door to the apartment is no simple door - it's sheeted with iron, like a door to a vault.

"The apartment belongs to Yuriy's mother," Natalya says. "She works in Italy. After the Soviet Union collapsed, there was no law. The apartment was broken into three times, so she had this iron door installed."

After the Soviet Union fell, the new government of Ukraine sold individual apartments to the occupants, but the maintenance of hallways, elevators, and grounds was left for an apartment dwellers' committee to hire someone. Judging from the dusty gloom of the hallway, the plan doesn't work that well.

The iron door opens and Yuriy greets us. He speaks softly to Natalya and she translates. He has a gentle face, dark curly hair and glasses. Natalya tells us he is a lawyer and that he works at the university.

To Find Myhailo

The parquet floors of the apartment gleam, as do the mahogany pieces of furniture along the walls. Natalya shows us the room where we can rest after our showers and breakfast. Huge embroidered pillows cover a daybed laid out for us. Off from the kitchen, Yuriy has the table set with yogurts, boiled eggs, cucumbers, ham, crusty rolls, and coffee.

After our nap Yuriy suggests that rather than going to a hotel, we can be his guests. I say, "Why not?" We can pay Yuriy rather than give the money to a hotel. But that's not what he means. He wants us as guests, not paying customers. Natalya wants to spend the afternoon showing us the sites of Lviv. Tomorrow, Olya will take us to the village whose name somewhat adds to the east/west confusion of what it is to be Ukrainian.

"It's *Vovkhivsti*" Natalya says. "Not *Volkhivsti*. That's Russian. In Ukrainian, *Wolf Place* is *Vovkhivsti*."

Vovk - Ukrainian. *Volk* - Russian. *Wowkh* - Polish. Three spellings for *Wolf*. When my grandparents came to Manitoba, they came from *Volkhivsti*. The pronunciation changed to *Vovkhivsti* only after the fall of the Soviet Union and the establishment of an independent Ukraine. *Vovk*, not *Volk!*

Yuriy goes to his computer where he finds two villages with the name *Vovkhivsti*. Olya will take us to the one that's nearest Borschiv. I had told Natalya that my relatives in Canada had said that the village was close to Borschiv.

If Sofiya's tour in Kyiv showed the Russian hand on Ukraine, the afternoon with Natalya in Lviv showed us what had once been a strong Polish presence. Mausoleums on the rolling hills of the city's famous cemetery contain the remains of Polish aristocrats. There are some Red Army officers buried here, but the Polish mausoleums dominate.

Ukranian icon, Ivan Franko's grave is here. His headstone is a bare-chested Franko wielding a pick-axe - a sculpture carved in the Stalinist style of socialist realism. I ask an attendant when it was erected. He says he doesn't know, but he thinks it was in the 1930s.

Franko died in poverty, his corpse then dressed in rags and laid out on a table. A professor told his Ukrainian students: "Go and see him lying - as poor as your entire nation is. You did not prize him when he was alive, and you do not prize him now, when he is dead." His friends then buried Franko in the Polish cemetery.

This was in 1916 when Austria was at war. After the war Lviv came under Polish rule. The cemetery attendant had said "Sometime in the 1930s...?"

It's inconceivable that Polish officials would have allowed the erection of a grandiose Franko monument. At the time of the Warwaruk immigration to Canada, Ivan Franko was the most famous writer of Ukrainian nationalism in Halychyna. The city named after him, *Ivano-Frankivsk,* is not far from Vovkhivsti. It's certain now that in Ukraine's new era, a Lviv cemetery attendant is not going to acknowledge that the Soviets would have ever erected a statue of a famous Ukrainian Nationalist writer.

The railway station, completed in 1900, was built with three waiting rooms - first class for Polish landlords and Austrian government officials. Sunlight shines through a hundred window panes, and a hundred lightbulbs hang from two bronze chandeliers. The room has squared marble pillars, and walls panelled with dark oak. The second class waiting room was for merchants and bankers, including mostly Jews. The third class room, not nearly as ornate as the other two, was for the departing peasants.

To Find Myhailo

The next morning, Olya takes us to the bus station. Yuriy says it will be a five hour ride to Chortkiv. We are to stay overnight there, as there'll be no hotels in the village.

Mavis and I wait on a bench outside, while Olya goes into the bus station for tickets. After some moments, a rather husky man sitting beside me stands up to face us. The open collar of his white cotton shirt exposes a delicate chain with a little cross pendant. The shirt has a narrow embroidered stripe that runs down from his left shoulder. In his left hand he holds a two-litre bottle of *kvass,* a fermented beverage made from bread.

"Where you from?" he asks in broken English.

"Canada," I answer, "And you?"

"Here in Ukraine."

"But your English is good."

"I work two years in Ireland," he says. "My name is Anatole."

I sit beside him on the bus all the way to Chortkiv. He's a truck dispatcher, and having completed a few days work in Lviv, he's on his way home to Chernivsti. Anatole says it's good for him to talk to me because he likes to practice his English. For five hours we talk nonstop, and I learn much about Halychyna. Every village we pass through has a Red Army Memorial in the style of socialist realism - a giant soldier, some with two - a male and female, some with several soldiers on the attack. The monuments are etched with the names of those from the village who fought and died in the war. Every monument has shreds of withered flowers at its base, remnants of this spring's May 9th anniversary of Victory Day - the Red Army's taking of Berlin.

"Only old people put those flowers," Anatole says. "But have a look!"

He points to one of the many newly constructed shrines we've seen along the way, every one of them strewn with wreaths of fresh flowers, each shrine mounted with a cross, and a black and red flag.

"For the Ukrainian heroes," Anatole says. "The fighters for Ukrainian Independence. For Stepan Bandera. For the Ukrainian Patriotic Army who fought the Russian Communists. And the people themselves pay. Put up the shrines. The Government pays nothing."

The bus stops for twenty minutes in Chortkiv. Anatole gets off with us to make sure we don't pay too much for a taxi, and he tells the driver to take us to a good hotel that's not expensive. He has already given me his phone number, and he tells me that if we ever come to Ukraine again, that I make sure to call him. He and his wife will take us camping in the Carpathian Mountains.

The desk clerk looks as young as Olya. She tells us that the rooms are nearly filled with Polish tourists, but there's still two rooms left. One with three beds, and the other with two.

"We can all sleep in one room," Olya says.

I tell Olya to ask how we'd get to Vovkhivsti in the morning. The clerk tells us that her husband can take us. He's going there tomorrow. I want to know how much it would cost, and she says he'll do it for nothing. But I insist that we should pay him something. She shrugs, phones him, then tells Olya he'll take thirty hryvnia, which is about four dollars. Our room with three beds is about thirty dollars.

We eat at the hotel's patio restaurant, open to the street. We're the only ones, except for three young men seated at a table across from us. One of them goes into the kitchen and comes back out with half a bottle of vodka. Olya laughs.

"He says he's going to drink the vodka all by myself." He scurries to another table. But his companions follow. A moment later, two other men who appear slightly older than the trio, join them from off the street.

"Those two are Polish," Olya whispers.

We're halfway through our meal when a St. Bernard dog steps up onto the patio and heads for our table. The lad with the vodka bottle whistles, and he throws the dog a crust of bread. Our waitress comes out of the kitchen waving a slice of ham and the dog jumps at it, nearly knocking her down. A cook rushes out from the kitchen waving a spatula. Another cook yells in her high-pitched voice, "Shoo! Shoo!" The dog eats the ham then wanders across the patio out to the street on the other side.

We finish our meal, and before we leave, I walk over to the cooks who are sitting at a table drinking tea. Using a few Ukrainian words that I know, I thank them for the good food. I try to think of Ukrainian words to ask the young man if he drank all the vodka himself, but before I get the chance, one of the Polish men stands up and extends his hand.

"I am Polish professor," he says, then struts away from me to our table. He bows to Olya and in the same motion, grabs her hand and kisses it. I see fear in her eyes.

"Let's go," I tell Mavis and Olya. The three of us brush by the Polish professor, and we leave him standing with his hand extended in empty space.

In our room Olya has her ear to the door.

"They're arguing," she says. "The Polish man wants to beat up on you."

The lock on the door is broken and Mavis wants me to push my bed up against it.

"That's crazy," I tell her, and then she props a chair against the doorknob.

"What good will that do?"

"At least we'll hear them," she says.

Olya wants to go to another hotel. I get the impression that the three Ukrainians are telling the two Poles to leave us alone, but whatever the case, Olya's in no way indifferent to the commotion. Fortunately their arguments soon stop, and it's not long until we're settled in for a good night's sleep.

The desk clerk's husband is a beer salesman, and he has calls to make in several villages. Vovkhivsti's his first stop. He can drop us off there, and pick us up in the evening on his way back. If we're going to find relatives, it'll have to be today. Olya has a meeting with her English professor tomorrow afternoon at the Ivan Franko University in Lviv.

On the way to Vovkhivsti, Olya tells the beer salesman about our incident with the Polish professor.

"That's not surprising," he says. "Every summer, hundreds of these guys come here. They think Chortkiv is their city. They come to drink cheap vodka, chase Ukrainian girls, and beat up foreigners."

I assume from this that some of the Polish families have not forgotten that they once owned this place, and that by considering themselves superior to Ukrainian peasants, some Polish men, like the professor, feel they have a free hand with Ukrainian girls. When my grandparents left this land, the Poles owned much of it. Do they think they'll get it back?

In the distance on one side of the road, the Soviet yellow of an abandoned collective farm building fades in the sun. On the other side of the road, rising out of the centre of a green forest, the golden dome of a church glistens.

To Find Myhailo

Just as we enter the valley, we pass by a large building that houses two Belarus combines. The building's in a yard that used to belong to the village's collective farm. Beyond the yard, a vast field of wheat stretches to the horizon. At least somebody is farming this land - not like many of the abandoned fields we've seen along the way.

Once into the village we stop in front of a little store - a trailer, much like you'd see on a construction site. The young store clerk has not heard of Warwaruks, but she points to an old woman sorting through a stack of blouses. "Warwaruk? Yes, yes, I know Warwaruks! I know where the oldest Warwaruk lives!" She rips a flap from a cardboard box, and taking a pencil from the clerk, draws a map to show our driver how to get there.

Vovkhivsti is a village of about a thousand people. A main street runs a little more than a mile from east to west. I'm soon to learn that before the war, fifteen Jewish families and forty Polish families lived along the west end. The Jews attended their synagogue in nearby Borschiv, but the Poles had their own Roman Catholic Church right here in Vovkhivsti. But by 1948, the Jews and Poles were gone, and the Polish church was salvaged for its building stones to build Ukrainian barns. A Polish Roman Catholic Church still stands in nearby Borschiv, but not the synagogue.

We make a right turn up a hill towards the Ukrainian Catholic Church, and turn right again into an alley with fenced-in yards on each side of us. House after house have flowers growing in their front yards. We hear dogs barking in the backyards. Most are chained, and in these same backyards we see chickens, ducks, and geese. In a small shed a cow munches hay. Which yard is Warwaruk's?

I yell out, "Warwaruk," and a man appears, pointing to a house further up the lane.

We stand at a porch entry, facing an elderly couple. Ustenna is short and frail, her large babushka tied so that it nearly hides her tiny wrinkled face. She wears a dark blue sweater that fully covers the top of her floral dress.

Petro has a stumpy appearance. He wears a white porkpie hat, light blue shirt, and baggy dark trousers. The look on his face is studied and thoughtful.

We are Warwaruks from Canada, and they are Warwaruks living in the home village in Ukraine. The name is probably common in Ukraine, but yet they are Warwaruks who live here in Vovkhivsti. My people came to Canada from Vovkhivsti. Tears come to my eyes.

I ask Petro if he knows of any Warwaruks who emigrated a hundred years ago. He says he doesn't know much about the family's past. Somebody went; maybe to Canada.

"My brother's wife might know," he says. "She takes more of an interest in family history." Petro sends his visiting grandson with us to show where the brother and his wife live.

"We are Warwaruks from Canada," we tell Vasyl and Maria at their porch entry. Vasyl greets us with an offer of vodka, and I try to explain that we don't drink alcohol. He goes back into the house and returns with a bottle of champagne. When we refuse this, Maria brings out a jar of what looks like water. Mavis doesn't want this because she doesn't know if the water is safe. Maria explains to Olya that it is birch juice. Every March, they tap the birch trees - they have at least a hundred litres of this juice. In Soviet times they were required to tap a thousand litres for the Collective.

To Find Myhailo

"We mixed half water," Vasyl says, "and they didn't know the difference."

We accept the time-honoured tradition to take a drink, and we find the taste to be mildly sweet, and delicately delicious.

Our driver sees that we are being looked after, so he tells Olya he'll drive the grandson back to Petro's, then head for the several villages he has to call on. He'll be back to pick us up at 7:30.

Vasyl and Maria's daughter and granddaughter will be here this afternoon from Ternopil. Tomorrow there is to be a big celebration at the church. Something about the 200th anniversary of the sighting of the Virgin Mary. Several thousand people will be here. Unfortunately, we won't be able to stay for the celebrations because of Olya's meeting.

As for my question of who went to Canada a hundred years ago, Vasyl's wife knows. Petro and Vasyl's grandfather was Fedor, and Maria knows that a hundred years ago, his brother, Danylo, my great grandfather, emigrated to Canada. I look carefully at Vasyl, and he studies me. We look for resemblances.

By the early afternoon, the daughter and granddaughter have arrived. The daughter, Helena, scurries back and forth from an out-building that is her mother's kitchen, loading the dinner table with food - sausage, cold chicken, rabbit, cured ham, tomatoes, cucumbers, apples, cottage cheese... Vasyl again offers us the vodka and champagne, and then he shrugs and pours the birch juice. We eat, and then Helena serves us a delicious torte she has brought with her from Ternopil. Maria simply watches. And as I watch Helena, I can't help but think of an old aunt of mine in

Canada, forty years ago, very pretty with her blond hair and squinting blue eyes - the very image of this Helena, with the same take charge hustle and bustle.

The granddaughter, Tetiana, is the same age as Olya, and just like Olya, she's an English major; her university is at Ternopil. Olya tells Tetiana about the encounter with the Polish professor, and says that she doesn't want to spend another night at the hotel in Chortkiv. Tetiana tells her that we can catch a bus tonight in Chortkiv that will take us to Ternopil. She'll phone her father - we can spend the night at their place in Ternopil.

Our beer salesman comes back to pick us up at 7:30 in the evening. He says that he has one more stop at another village, but in the meantime he can take us to the bus station in Chortkiv to wait for the 9 o'clock bus. Or if we want, we can ride along with him to the other village and still have enough time to catch our bus. We choose the second option. Olya wants no part of having to sit waiting for a bus in Chortkiv. Not with Polish men leering at her.

All goes well until a tire goes flat. Slawa's car is a rusted 1980 Lada. He takes a bald, over-sized tire from the trunk, and a wrench made with a socket welded onto a piece of re-bar. It seems that he's not quite sure which way to turn the wrench, but either way, the rusted wheel nuts won't budge. I take a try, thinking, *leftie loosie, rightie tightie*. I kick at the wrench, to the left, but still the frozen nuts won't budge.

The time is 8:40, and it will take at least twenty minutes to get to Chortkiv. Our bus leaves at 9:00.

Slawa talks on his cell phone, and in minutes a car races toward us. A young man gets out, laughs at Slawa's wrench, and with his own tools quickly changes the tire. I

To Find Myhailo

offer him some money. He won't take it so I stuff a twenty hryvna bill into his shirt pocket.

Over broken pavement our beer salesman races to Chortkiv. At each bump on the road, the over-sized spare scrapes on rusted metal. Slawa says that if the bus has already left, he will chase it down.

"Look!" Olya says as we near the bus station. "It's our bus!" Slawa pulls up right in front of it so it can't move. He talks to the driver. Is there room for us?

Olya translates. "Standing room only."

"We'll stand!" Mavis says.

As we wait for our tickets, Olya has pushed her way into the aisle. In moments, she reappears.

"Three seats!" she says. "Right at the back!"

We ride all the way to Ternopil in the plush rear seats of a first-class Polish bus. Near midnight, the three of us cram into a dark elevator that clinks and clanks its way up to Tetiana's parents' apartment. I knock on a wooden door and Tetiana's father invites us in.

Before we go to bed, Stefan treats us to slices of Helena's torte. Olya will sleep in Tetiana's room, and Mavis and I have the daybed in a living-room filled with flowering plants. In the morning Stefan serves breakfast highlighted with more torte, and then he takes us with him on the way to his workplace. He will show us where to catch the bus that will take us to Lviv.

Sofiya has arrived back from Kyiv where she had been applying for a visa to sing at a Ukrainian festival in New York. She was denied, but Mavis and I will hear her sing. She's taking us to an outdoor concert and youth camp-out in a valley on the outskirts of Lviv.

Hundreds of young people camp on the hillside. Tents are everywhere, along with blue and yellow flags, and the black and red of Stepan Bandera. A Ukrainian rock star sings on the stage on the valley floor. Ukrainian dance. Flowers. The art of Ukrainian politics. Sofiya sings on the stage.

The main feature of this camp-out is the giant screen. It shows war-games. Cadets in army fatigues carry flags, swing on ropes, aim rifles at targets, crawl on their hands and knees.

"Recruiting?" I ask Sofiya when she joins us back on the hillside.

"No, no," she says. "Just showing the fun the young people have at the summer and weekend camp-outs."

But it's clear to me. The young people shown on the big screen are being trained for warfare. On the bus to Chortkiv, Anatole had pointed out the many Ukrainian Patriotic Army Memorials. He told me that his son attends youth-group camp-outs in the traditions of Bandera. This would be the army of the future. He told me that the present Ukrainian army is a joke. I could see that the youngsters filmed in these war-games were being trained to follow in the footsteps of Stepan Bandera.

To Find Myhailo

CHAPTER 3

*The lanes and yards of Vovkhivsti are
like Glenavon's, years ago.
Chickens in my back alley when I was five.
The alley is the place of my Kite and Cuckoo dream...
In this alley the Glenavon Massey-Harris Dealer
chopped the heads off chickens.
They ran askew, spastic necks
spraying the alley dirt with blood...
On this second visit to Vovkhivsti
I hear about Myhailo...*

It is 2009; we're on our way again to see the Warwaruks in Vovkhivsti. Stefan and Helena, with daughter Tetiana are taking us. Several times a year they go to fill their car with vegetables, sausage, bacon, eggs, ducks, and chickens to take back to their apartment in Ternopil.

We pass by a village with its Red Army granite soldier memorial. I see the list of names, and the withered shreds of flowers placed a month ago on Victory Day.

Fresh flowers adorn the Ukrainian Patriotic Army shrines - more monuments than we saw in 2007. Every village has one, with its Virgin Mary, the flag of Bandera, the gold and blue of Ukraine, and the etched list of names.

We pass traffic safety monuments - a wrecked automobile mounted high on a pole. The Soviet age pavement is cracked and broken. Cars are new. Russian *Ladas*, and German *Opels*.

We see new churches, and on a knoll, the brown and broken boards creak on an abandoned windmill. A woman draws water from an open well. We see far in the distance a large field of red poppies, and then another that looks to be a thousand acres or more of wheat. Other fields appear abandoned, grown over with weeds.

Down a spreading hillside lies the village of Vovkhivsti - bright-coloured houses - backyards filled with chickens, ducks and geese. We see the open well we saw before, with its long pole aimed skyward like the neck of a crane.

We sit at a table in the backyard of the Warwaruks, who in 2007 brought tears to my eyes. Petro seems careful with his breathing. He doesn't gasp, but his every word takes its time. Ustenna hands him a plastic monitor which he clamps on his thumb, reads the numbers, then hands the monitor back to his wife. Tetiana translates.

To Find Myhailo

"My father, Myhailo, was foreman on a Polish farm. He kept the horses. Like Grandfather Fedor before him, he tanned hides." I had heard parts of the story before: the Warwaruk family made leather boots and coats.

In 1894, Danylo Warwaruk was one of the nine founders of Vovkhivsti's Ukrainian youth group, *Prosvita*. Six years later, benevolent Austrian Rule allowed for a Ukrainian school in the village. Before her family emigrated to Canada, my grandmother on my mother's side, starting at the age of six, spent three years learning to read in this school.

In 1932, Polish Rule closed the Ukrainian schools, but Myhailo successfully insisted that Vovkhivsti's remain open. He wanted his children to be educated in Ukrainian, and not Polish. Though he had only two years of formal schooling himself, he spoke four languages: Russian, Polish, German, along with his native Ukrainian.

"Your great-grandfather in Canada sent money to help build a hall," Petro says. "Prosvita had a plaque put up with his name on it."

"It's still there?"

"No one knows what happened to it," Petro says. "And there is no more hall. Some stone steps, that's all. The plaque's gone somewhere. Who knows."

In Manitoba I've seen the site of Danylo's homestead. A collapsed building still exists - the remains of the Don Hall. In the 1930s my father taught in Don School, half a mile from the hall. He directed plays for the stage on which my mother did Ukrainian dance. My grandmother, the one who could read and write Ukrainian, tramped barefoot in puddles of clay, straw, and horse manure to mix the mortar that chinked the logs for this hall. Seven years earlier Danylo had sent the money to help build a similar hall in

Vovkhivsti. He must certainly have been interested in the nurturing of Ukrainian language and culture. A culture distinct from the Polish? Did he distinguish from the Russian? Not far from Danylo's homestead in Manitoba, the collapsed building of the Volga store and post office still exists. The post office opened in 1912. Before that, anyone who had been to Winnipegosis would drop the mail off at Danylo's. His older son, Stefan, was the first postmaster. The Ukrainian district of my Canadian ancestors had their store, post office, hall, and school, named after rivers in Russia. I think that Danylo's money sent to Vovkhivsti was for a hall meant to resist the forces of Polish domination, not Russian. At that time I don't think my ancestors made much of an issue over whether they were Russian or Ukrainian, as long as they weren't considered to be Poles. But by 1939, Halychyna was no longer an eastern province of Poland. Vovkhivsti became a village in the new Ukrainian People's Republic in the Soviet Union.

In early 1940, the villagers met with Soviet representatives sent out from Kyiv. The people met in their village hall, a gathering place with Prosvita rules that Ukrainians should marry only Ukrainians, and that they should stay out of Jewish taverns. This hall would soon see a major transformation. Pictures of Lenin and Stalin would replace religious icons. The *hall* that had been a place to read books, became a *club* for political indoctrination, dancing, and drinking vodka.

At this 1940 meeting the villagers learned that their local Soviet government was to be centred in nearby Borschiv. Thirty surrounding villages were to send representatives to sit on this Soviet Council. Petro said that Vovkhivsti chose Myhailo. I had always heard that Soviet

To Find Myhailo

elections usually had only one name on the ballot. I don't know if this was how Myhailo was elected, but I learn much later that very few of the villagers would want this job.

I ask Petro, "Was Myhailo a communist?"

"No, not a communist. My father was a community leader," Petro says. "A public speaker with his four languages." Petro tells me that his father had leadership experience as foreman on the Polish farm. At seeding and harvest, other Ukrainians worked for Myhailo. They trusted him to represent their village. And then Petro grins.

"I remember," he says, "Father brought sausage home for us children, every week from the Borschiv Soviet."

I ask about *Holodomor,* the starvation of millions of Ukrainians due to Stalin's collectivization of agriculture in the early 30s.

"Not here," Petro says. "Vovkhivsti was still part of Poland then."

"But 1946 we had famine," Ustenna says.

"A poor crop in 1946," Petro says. "Everybody buried what little grain they managed to harvest, because the *komsomol,* the *young communists,* were coming from Ternopil with iron probes. They demanded our grain to feed the Red Army that was still fighting the Bandera insurgents. They didn't find our grain, but ten people in the village died from starvation."

That same autumn, OUN-UPA sent a message to the villagers in western Ukraine: *Soon the Bolsheviks will conduct the grain levy. Anyone among you who brings grain to the collection points will be killed like a dog, and your entire family butchered.*

"The komsomol didn't find our wheat," Ustenna says. "A starving boy from another village came begging. We gave him some." She, too, tells us that ten people in the village starved to death. Hunger was so bad that some people ate dead babies.

"How many people in your village?"

"Three hundred families in Vovkhivsti," Petro says. "Before the war, forty of these were Polish, and fifteen were Jewish. Now there are only Ukrainians."

In the summer of 1941, the Nazi invasion of Ukraine commenced under the code name of *Operation Barbarossa*. It was winter when the Germans got to Vovkhivsti.

"Soldiers in the house," Petro says, "And us boys ran out barefoot in the snow."

The Germans didn't stay in Vovkhivsti. They were satisfied that the villagers were on their side. Prosvita supported the Germans. The German army simply arranged for the collection of provisions, and then continued its march to the east. They kept Myhailo as mayor, or as Ukrainians would say, *village head*. Had he been a communist, the Germans would likely have shot him. Ukrainian communists were exterminated, just like the Jews.

German rule continued in Vovkhivsti until April of 1944. Starting in January, they began their preparations for retreat. Part of this was to gather up Vovkhivsti's Jews.

I ask, "German soldiers did this?"

"No," Petro says. "Ukrainian militia."

"From Vovkhivsti?"

"No," Petro says. "They came from Borschiv." He tells me that they came and took the Jews to Borschiv. They were shot there, and buried in a mass grave along with two thousand Jews from surrounding villages.

Petro tells us that his mother and grandmother were good friends of Sosia Flintenstein, a Jewish woman who worked with them in the village office. Only much later, on our 5th visit to the village, six years later, did we learn that

To Find Myhailo

Tetiana's translation got some of this information mixed up. Actually, Sosia Flintenstein was from the Soviet office in Borschiv. A woman by the name of Solomon did housecleaning for this woman. When news of the arrests came, Sosia fled from Borschiv to seek refuge in Vovkhivsti.

Along the south edge of the village, close by the Jewish street, there is an underground tunnel that used to be a kerosene warehouse. The Solomon woman, who did cleaning for the Jewish woman, lived in a house that sat on top of the tunnel's entry. Sosia Flintenstein and her fourteen year-old son hid in this tunnel for eighteen months. Throughout this period Myhailo's wife and mother helped by supplying them with bread and cheese and other provisions.

In April of 1944, the Germans retreated from the village, but first they burned the houses. Myhailo was able to save his. He persuaded the German soldiers to spare it because the children were inside. When the Soviets returned, Myhailo continued on as village head until the summer of the following year.

"Ten weeks after Easter," Petro says. "Bandits took him." He was never seen again. I ask if these bandits were members of the nationalist insurgents - the UPA, the Ukrainian Patriotic Army.

"I don't know," he says. "There were many bands hiding in the forest, some of them UPA, some of them just bandits."

He goes on to tell me that in 1967, the family thought they had found Myhailo's remains. Bones had been found in a well. Some of the Warwaruk family wanted a Red Flag Funeral, but others insisted it be Catholic. As it turned out, they didn't have to make a final decision. A villager came forward to say that he had seen who had been thrown in the well – it was someone much younger than Myhailo.

"Hard on your breathing," Ustenna says, "No more talk." She hands Petro his monitor.

In Vasyl and Maria's backyard, their son-in-law, Stepan, washes his new Lada car. Helena's in the house, helping her mother make up the bed in the living room where Mavis and I will sleep. We're sitting with Vasyl on a bench up against the house. Tetiana translates.

We face the backyard with its chickens, ducks and geese. The backyard has rabbit pens, and a dilapidated outdoor toilet that hides behind an equally dilapidated shed. The toilet has a broken door that faces out to Vasyl and Maria's bountiful half-acre vegetable garden.

"I had a cousin," Vasyl says. "Maria Horbova. In 1949 in the winter, I was walking to school. By the hall I saw Maria hanging from a tree. She was nineteen."

Vasyl remembers her green sweater, black skirt, and her dangling bare feet. The talk was that Maria Horbova spied for the Red Army. In 1949 the war was still on in Vovkhivsti.

"I don't know," Vasyl says. "I think she was a little bit simple in the head."

Before we leave the village, Mavis and I go to the Red Army memorial. We see the name *Warwaruk,* along with the names *Budzay, Basaraba, Beyak, Solomon...* all Ukrainian names of families who came to Manitoba. *Warwaruk* appears twice. *Solomon* three times. *Basaraba* twice. My father's sister married a Basaraba. My great-grandfather Danylo is buried in a small Manitoba graveyard on the land my father's sister inherited. I looked for the grave, but to no avail. It had been plowed under to create more field on which to grow barley to feed cows.

To Find Myhailo

On the outskirts of Borschiv we stop to see the mound where Vovkhivsti's Jews are buried. A foundation from Israel has recently erected a monument to indicate that two thousand Jews are buried here, but the mound looks unattended, grown over with tall grass and weeds. A high brick wall blocks the view from the town, as if to show that this sight is not a part of Borschiv.

Anatole meets us at the bus station. He drives an Opel, a German car, and looks down his nose at Tetiana's father's car which brought us here. His car is a Russian Lada. Anatole looks down his nose at all things Russian. He in fact loathes the Russians. His grandparents had been landowners in Volynia, deported to Siberia in the 1930s.

We come across a Jewish museum in Toist, a village along the way to Anatole's home on the outskirts of Chernivsti. After having seen the burial mound in Borschiv, I want to see this museum.

"What for you want to know about Jews?" Anatole says. "Many Jews were Bolsheviks. I hate those communist bastards!"

The museum's on the front street. The building appears to be an old store, and through the display windows I see old photos and newspaper clippings. But the door's locked. By all appearances the museum has been closed for a long time.

To Find Myhailo

CHAPTER 4

Do I remember from my childhood the end of the war?
A bonfire on the Glenavon sports ground?
I have no memory of a Hitler scarecrow, but
an old friend says 'yes there was.'
I don't remember Hitler burning - I was two -
It was many years later
my friend told me about a Hitler burning on the
top of the fire...
He was a young boy with his father, the
Massey-Harris dealer.
They drove all over town in a truck
to gather wooden packing crates
and any other refuse that would burn.
This was shortly after the fall of Berlin...
A celebration.
Now in Lviv I see for sure,
clouds of smoke and flames...

In 2011 there are no baggage carousels in Lviv's Soviet-Era airport. To get our suitcases, Mavis and I cram into a room not much bigger than a prison cell. Mavis and at least another dozen travelers hunt through the pile of luggage, while I decide to step outside and find Natalya who's supposed to meet us. Red and yellow murals cover the airport walls - the Soviet Realism of three workers smelting iron, and a collective farm scene with two women carrying milk pails. In front of them on the mural a painted man leads two painted cows.

Lviv is the city's Ukrainian name. When these murals were painted it was the Russian *Lvov*. Before that, the Polish *Lwow*, and when the Austrians had the city built, it was *Lemberg*.

I see Natalya wave as she makes her way through the spaces between the taxi cabs parked out front. She gets to me just as Mavis appears lugging two suitcases. I quietly remind myself of having observed that it's the women who hoe the gardens in Ukraine.

We take turns to hug Natalya.

"I got you a place to stay that's close to the Market Square," Natalya says. "Clean, and not expensive. We'll take a taxi. And don't you ask the driver how much is the fare. I will ask."

It's the 8th of May, 2011, and Mavis and I have once again arrived in Lviv, the city in western Ukraine that was part of Austria when my grandparents emigrated over a century ago. The 8th of May is the day before *Victory Day*, the holiday that Stalin declared to celebrate the Red Army's taking of Berlin.

But in Lviv, it is also the day before *City Day* - the Holy Day of St. George, Lviv's patron saint. A man tells me this as we get off the plane. He has been to a Rotary Club meeting in Paris, and he says that we have picked an exciting weekend to come to his city. Traditionally, City Day had been held in early May. However, at the end of WWII, Stalin declared that it be held in the fall, so as not to conflict with the Red Army's victory. But then with the collapse of the Soviet Union, and the achievement of Ukraine's Independence, Lviv's municipal council restored the May date.

The man also tells us about the *Cross of St. George*. During the centuries of Tsarist Russia, the Cross of St. George was the medal worn by soldiers of the tsar's Imperial Army. But in 1917, the Russian Revolution took place, and the victorious Bolsheviks got rid of the medal. Lenin wouldn't be pinning something religious on a Red Army soldier's lapel. However, after the fall of the Soviet Union, and a despairing decade of a demoralized Russia, the Country's new President, Vladimir Putin, in his attempts at restoring some old glory, brought back the medal for Red Army Veterans to wear on Victory day. It is a cross of two ribbons, both striped orange and black. Putin also declared that the red flag with its hammer and sickle could be flown for the celebrations.

These changes have been very well received throughout Russia, but they present a major problem for Ukraine. Many Ukrainian Nationalists, followers of Stepan Bandera, fought against the Red Army, especially in the western part of the country. But on the other hand, many were loyal Red Army soldiers, like my Warwaruk relatives. Veterans and their families hold on to the memories of the war - the sacrifices these Ukrainians made with their blood for the Red Army's victory over Nazi Germany.

But Lviv's municipal council, vociferously anti-Russian, passed two more by-laws: that it be against the law to fly the red flag with its hammer and sickle on City Day, and against the law to wear the Cross of *St. George*. For Ukrainians in Lviv, St. George's Day is something very special. The centuries old Ukrainian Catholic cathedral that overlooks the city is named after St. George. It is the greatest of insults to have Russians usurp the city's Holy symbols.

The next day, Natalya takes us to Lviv's central square, the old *Rynok* market place built over a hundred years ago in the majestically classic style of the Austrian Empire. Beer tents are set up throughout the square, and below a looming statue of Taras Shevchenko, the national poet of Ukraine, several Ukrainian Catholic priests and scores of worshipers sing in prayer. A *Svoboda* Party member hands out leaflets. Another member speaks out loudly to the crowd.

I ask Natalya, "Where are the Victory Day celebrations?"

"At the Red Army Memorial," she says. "We won't go. There'll be trouble."

But I insist. We get on a crowded trolley bus that takes us to the famous Polish *Lychakivski* Cemetery, and the site of the Red Army Memorial. Where we get off, women are selling bouquets of flowers. Old men dressed in Red Army uniforms of grey wool stand about, medals of the Cross of St. George pinned to their lapels. We join the crowd moving along a walkway towards the Memorial.

Suddenly, several young men dressed in black and wearing masks - a tight red knit on one side of the face, and black on the other - climb down from a trolley bus. More young men, some of them bare-faced, some totally covered in black, one flying the black and red Stepan Bandera flag, race about, darting here and there, confronting the uniformed veterans by ripping the orange and black ribbons from their lapels. Four of the young men circle and shove at

To Find Myhailo

a grey-haired old man. Another demonstrator grabs a young woman's bouquet of flowers.

We hear what sounds like firecrackers, and see clouds of smoke and flames on a hillside above and to the side of the Memorial - burning red flags, and smoke bombs hurled at the Red Army veterans below, and at the old women who are likely the widows of men who had fought in *The Great Patriotic War,* and maybe some of the women had fought in it themselves. And there are younger people, both men and women, attempting to place their wreaths and bouquets.

"Up here," Natalya says. "Out of the way!" We climb up an embankment that overlooks the walkway.

"Those red flags," Natalya says, "A busload from Crimea brought them. Provocateurs."

From this upper vantage point both Mavis and I feel much safer. We are above the turmoil, watching, Mavis with her camera taking a video of the lines of riot police with their helmets, shields, and batons opposing what looks to be hundreds of young men dressed in black, some wearing the black and red masks, rushing about, running at the police, then retreating as the police swing their batons. From the hillside that overlooks the Memorial, the black-clad demonstrators spit at the wreath layers.

A demonstrator runs by us, his head covered with blood. "See what the Yanukovych police do!" he yells.

Some years ago, on Canada's Remembrance Day, Mavis and I attended the Canadian Legion's ceremony at the Cenotaph in Saskatoon. Many veterans stood in line, smartly dressed in their grey flannels, tams on their heads, and the glitter of medals on the lapels of their navy blue blazers. I cannot imagine medals being ripped off the chests of these old men at the Saskatoon Cenotaph.

We visit a prison that's now a museum. Because Natalya is a friend of the director, we get to see areas not yet open to the public. Water stains blotch the basement walls, and pieces of fallen plaster litter the floor. The stuccoed walls and floor of a solitary confinement cell have pieces of broken glass etched into the concrete.

"A prisoner could not lie down." the director says. "Or lean against a wall."

Another cell has padded leather walls, the colour of rust and dirty streaks of black and yellow.

"For beatings," the director says. "A padded wall leaves no marks."

During the time of Polish rule, Ukrainian nationalists were locked up in this prison. When the Soviets took over, their special police, the NKVD, ran the place, and many more nationalists were rounded up and crammed into crowded cells - one square meter of floor allotted to each prisoner.

In the basement, along with the torture cells, is the interrogation room. A green stool looks tiny where it sits in front of a large oak desk. The chair behind the desk is much higher than the stool. A leather strap hangs from a coat rack.

The Germans took Lviv in July of 1941. The Soviets fled, but before they left, they shot and buried the Ukrainian nationalists in the prison courtyard.

I ask the director about the thousands of Jews who perished in the pogrom that took place that July. Some historians say they were slaughtered even before the Germans arrived.

"NKVD," the director says. "Peoples' Commissariat for Internal Affairs. They arranged it all. Before they fled, they set free the criminals who were thieves and murderers - the ones who weren't political prisoners. The NKVD told them to kill Jews."

To Find Myhailo

Only fools and children tell the truth?
I tell the director about Myhailo Warwaruk's death. I tell him that when I had visited the family in 2009, they told me that insurgents from the Ukrainian Patriotic Army had killed Myhailo.

"Impossible," the director says. "They were likely NKVD agents posing as members of UPA. Or they may have been common bandits, but not UPA."

I'm struck by his certainty.

The following morning, Natalya and Yuriy drop us off in Ternopil. From there we go by train to Kyiv with Tetiana and her mother, Helena. Petro Warwaruk's daughter, Olga, lives in Kyiv. Just like Helena, Olga is Myhailo's granddaughter, and also, just like Helena, she knows very little about him. In Soviet Ukraine, parents divulged very little, if any information about past events that could be deemed controversial.

Helena takes charge in Olga's kitchen, serving us poppyseed rolls and pouring tea. Olga talks, and Tetiana translates.

"To go to university," Olga says, "You had to be a member of the Young Communist League."

She smiles - a sheepish look. "In high school, I was komsomol secretary."

I ask about her grandfather's death.

"I have a friend in Italy who might know something. She grew up in Vovkhivsti. At university she wrote a paper on the village's history."

Olga calls her up on Skype.

"NKVD killed your grandfather," the woman says. "Your father, Petro, told me."

I'm puzzled, because in 2009, Petro told me that it was either UPA, or bandits, who had killed Myhailo. I can't ask Petro now, for he had died in the spring.

Olga takes us to *Babi Yar,* a gorge that is the burial place of over two hundred thousand people. Though she has lived in Kyiv since 1991, she has never been to Babi Yar. A man who speaks Russian tells us that over 70% of the victims in Babi Yar were Jews. The executions commenced in the summer of 1941 when the Germans took Kyiv, and continued until their defeat at Stalingrad eighteen months later. Again, like at the time of the German advance on Lviv, there is the question of Ukrainian participation in the killing of Jews.

Throughout the Soviet era, the Russians never mentioned that Jews were killed at Babi Yar. In Soviet doctrine, it was the Soviet People who were exterminated. As for Ukrainian collaboration? On the internet, I find another instance of blame directed at the evils of the Soviet Secret Police. A website says that the pictures of the Ukrainian gunmen standing with SS officers on the lip of the gorge were NKVD agents posing as Ukrainians.

We visit the *Victims of Holodomor Museum.*

Sculptures of grieving angels bow at the entrance, and the starving little girl statue greets us with her solitary wheat spikelet that Stalin would have punished her for had she been caught picking it up from the ground. Inside the museum are martyr books with the names of millions who starved from the Bolshevik taking of the grain, first in the 1922 civil war, and again during the early 30s collectivization of agriculture in Ukraine.

To Find Myhailo

Tetiana, her mother, Mavis and I, take the night train back to Ternopil. On the way to Kyiv we had an enclosed sleeping compartment with two sets of bunks, but now there's nothing available. We'll have to settle for a sleeper with no doors.

Our tickets show the car number, and the number of our compartment. When we get to it, a shabbily dressed young man and woman sit on the bottom bunks. The top bunks are stuffed to the roof with bulging cloth bags.

"Gypsies," Helena says. She scolds them. "This is our compartment! And take your bags! They stink! This man's from Canada and he has asthma. He can't stand your stink!"

The woman says nothing; she simply glares. After a long moment, the man, and then the woman, get up and move down the aisle. In a few minutes the man comes for the bags. He finds storage space and what serves as a sleeping shelf above the windows.

Tetiana crawls up to the top bunk on one side of our compartment, her mother on the bottom bunk. I'm on the top on our side, Mavis on the bottom. Through the open doorway I see the Gypsy woman. She's directly across from us, on the shelf above the windows. She glares, then mutters something to Tetiana who starts to cry.

Tetiana gets down from her bunk and sobs on her mother's shoulder. They talk, the daughter crying as Helena holds her close. After a long while, Tetiana crawls back up to her bunk. She wraps into her blankets, quietly sobbing as the Gypsy woman gives her one more stare.

In the morning, Tetiana tells us: "The Gypsy said I was a bad woman, and she was going to hex me with a curse."

I wonder about folklore that my grandparents must have brought with them to Canada, a mystique not carried forward to my generation. But I remember something my mother told me about Gypsies in my hometown of Glenavon. They'd bring their midway to the Fair. A fortune teller read Mother's palm and told her she wouldn't have any more babies. I was the last one, and Mother was convinced that the Gypsy woman could see into the future. This took place when I was a little boy, but in Ukraine, at least with young Tetiana, the belief in the mystical powers of Gypsies is very much alive.

As they did in 2009, Stepan and Helen take us to Vovkhivsti in their Lada car. They will load up again with chickens and vegetables. On this visit, we walk down a lane, past several houses, to meet another son of Myhailo, the one who had wanted a Red Flag funeral when the family thought they had found Myhailo's bones. His name is Mykola. I'm confused with names. His father, Myhailo - his name, Mykola. There's Petro, Vasyl, and now this brother, Mykola. I learn there was even a fourth brother, the oldest, Ivan, no longer living, along with a sister, Anna.

I tell Vasyl and Mykola that Olga's friend said the NKVD killed their father - that Petro had told her this. Both brothers laugh. They know exactly who apprehended Myhailo. In 1945, ten Fridays after Easter, five members of UPA held court all through the night. Vasyl and Mykola name them - three women - a *Hanna, Sonya,* and *Ustena;* and two men - an *Ivan,* and *Dmitro.* They found Myhailo guilty of collusion with the enemy and sentenced him to death. They kept him in the house all the next day, and the following night took him to the forest.

To Find Myhailo

The NKVD later captured and shot the insurgent, Ivan. Dmitro was sent to Siberia, never to return. Records show that Dmitro's brother, Vasyl, was involved. He survived by moving to another village and changing his name. I don't know what happened to the three women.

Once again, just like in 2009, the final part of our Ukraine tour is with Anatole. He meets us in Borschiv to take us to his home near Chernivsti. On the way we stop at a museum in Kosiv.

Half of this majestic building contains artifacts of Hutzul Ukrainians, the folklore dwellers of the Carpathians. The other half tells the story of UPA, and how these fighters for Ukrainian independence sought refuge in the nearby mountain hillsides. As we are leaving the building I discover what I consider to be a far bigger story - the woman at the desk quietly tells us that the museum had once been the home of the Rabbi of Kosiv. Directly across the street, is an equally grand structure, newly built. It's the town hall, built where Kosiv's synagogue stood before it was destroyed. Further uphill, and back out of sight, is an ancient Jewish cemetery.

The ironwork fence looks new, and beyond it, ancient gravestones are scattered helter-skelter in a mass of overgrown grass and shrubbery. But there are two new structures: blue-painted iron pipes support the metal roofs of two tent-like enclosures, each surrounded by more of the shrub and grass wilderness. Each structure has a *Star of David* at the front, and both are fenced with black ironwork, and a horizontal diamond pattern of white metal piping. These are graves of two important rabbis of the past.

What was the original state of this overgrown cemetery? What has been vandalized? What has been pillaged? Who tends to the two iron-work structures?

Larry Warwaruk

A hillside of hardwood forest overlooks these two attended graves, as well as the scattered remains of the numerous unkempt gravestones poking every which way out of the overgrown tangles of grass. Hidden in a clearing high above in the middle of the forest, hulks a rough stone memorial at the site of a mass grave, similar to the one we saw on the outskirts of Borschiv. An inscription in Ukrainian reads:

In eternal memory of the Jews of Kosov and its surroundings, murdered here by the Nazi hangmen and their henchmen. 1941-1942. I notice the Russian spelling of Kosiv. This monument must have been erected before Ukraine's Independence.

Below this, another inscription reads in Hebrew:
In eternal memory of the Jews of Kosov and its surroundings who were murdered here by the Nazi murderers and their helpers (may their names be blotted out) in the years 1941-1942.

The Hebrew lettering has been scratched over.

We are not the only ones interested in this Jewish cemetery. Back at the front gate and iron-work fence, we meet a man dressed in Hutzul vest and hat that have all the colours of a flower garden. With him are a young Jewish man from Poland, and a married couple. They'd been at a function in the Carpathians - at a school - an agricultural institute that had taken on the name of the woman's grandfather. He had been an agrologist there, before the war when the Polish government sent him to the Carpathians to show Hutzuls the farming methods practiced in the Swiss Alps.

The woman is Jewish, and her husband, a German writer. During the war his father had been a Nazi SS officer. After the war he committed suicide. The Jewish woman's agrologist grandfather perished at Auschwitz.

Further on the way to Anatole's we stop at several war memorials; some of them Soviet Red Army, and some of them UPA, often side by side. There are many more UPA memorials than we saw in 2009, and any inscription on Soviet memorials that mentions fighting for the Soviet Motherland has been scratched out.

Further on we pass by a church, and then hundreds of gravestones on each side of the road.

"Have a look," Anatole says. "What the Soviets did. Built the highway right through the middle of the cemetery. Do you know, every year there is a car accident here. Somebody is killed every year! Just like near Lviv. The Soviets used Jewish gravestones for the base of a highway. And now, every year, somebody killed!"

Larry Warwaruk

*My mother's grandmother,
Danylo's daughter,
told my mother a story about Rusalka mermaids.
They swam on the ocean waves
when Warwaruks crossed
on a ship to Canada.
My mother's grandmother
knew the folk tales of these Rusalkas
who sat on the rocks on the shores
of Carpathian streams.
They lured young men
to join them in the water
where they tickled them to death.*

To Find Myhailo

Before the First World War, Ivan Franko foreshadowed Ukrainian animosity towards Jews. In the novel, Fateful Crossroads, a Jewish mayor... *introduces sidewalks, gas, and buses, creates parks and promenades, but in return for these good deeds mercilessly sucks dry the population of the city, empties the treasury, drains public sources of revenue, devastates forests, and sells off communally held land.*

Warwaruks crossed the ocean during the era that Franko wrote these words. How did my grandparents depict Jews? A Jewish store-keeper carried my mother's grandparents through their first year of settlement. My grandmother was nine years old. Her father was away to earn money pounding spikes on a Manitoba railroad. She and her mother stayed on at the homestead, cutting away brush and digging in the forest soil to prepare a garden patch for the coming spring. Through this first fall and winter they would rely on fish netted from the lake; bush partridges, rabbits, mushrooms, and high-bush cranberries taken from the forest; and flour, tea, salt, and matches they could charge at the store.

My grandmother's father had earned enough money to buy a milk cow, but the cow got sick. Her mother had to walk several miles through the forest to get medicine from Rabbi Gruber's country store. She had no money for the medicine, nor for the bag of flour that she had to carry on her back.

"Pay next year," the rabbi said. He even gave her free a bag of candy for her daughter who was waiting at the homestead, caring for a baby brother.

Was this something out of the ordinary, for a Jew to help out a poor Ukrainian? Ukrainians in Halychyna had five hundred years of dealing with Jews - some good deals, some bad. My ancestors came to Canada with this same tradition. My mother remembered the cattle-buyers from Winnipeg. In the doorway of her family's special east room with its icons of Christ, the Virgin Mary, various saints, and a portrait of Taras Shevchenko on the walls of plastered clay, stood my mother - a little girl peeking through a curtain. Two Hasidic Jews rocked back and forth on their heels. They wore prayer shawls and chanted prayers from little leather boxes called *phylacteries*. They had stayed overnight, and my mother remembered that her mother had sent her outside to gather eggs for the cattle-buyers' breakfast.

Though my grandmother did her best to support her husband's dealings with the outside English world, at the same time she stood fast against assimilation. Nearly all of her Manitoba neighbours were illiterate, but back in Vovkhivsti when she was six years old, she had attended the newly opened Prosvita school for Ukrainians. In three years she had learned how to read and write. She brought this skill with her to Manitoba, and after she married, she taught her eight children how to read and write in Ukrainian. When Presbyterian student missionaries came to the Don schoolhouse in the summer to teach the Ukrainian children English, she protested. She referred to these missionaries, as Jews! As far as my grandmother was concerned, the outside world was composed of Jews, Roman Catholic Poles, and Cree Indians whom she thought were Gypsies.

My grandmother, seated beneath the Taras Shevchenko portrait and the holy icons hanging from her plastered clay wall, taught Ukrainian literacy to her children. While she did this in Canada, in Halychyna the struggle for Ukrainian nationhood was in full swing. In 1924, A German Jew, Alfred Doblin, travelled through Halychyna to study Jewish life, so different from the urban Jewish culture of his Berlin. He wrote about Lviv when its name changed from the German *Lemberg* to the Polish *Lwow*. He wrote about Ukrainians in 1924 Halychyna:

The Ukrainians refuse to recognize the Polish reality of Lwow. The Ukrainian nation lives torn apart between the Russians and Poles, and peace is nowhere in sight... Many Ukrainians disgorge a terrible, blind, numb hatred, an entirely animal hatred of the Poles...

These feelings only strengthened after 1939, when Ukrainians in Halychyna added Russian communists to their hates - bolsheviks they equated with Jews.

Larry Warwaruk

*I remember the bronze plaque
on the wall in the Glenavon hall
with names of Canadian soldiers
from WW1 and WW11
all from Glenavon and area...
Mostly Englishmen.*

To Find Myhailo

Anatole says it is a great injustice that the veterans of the Ukrainian Insurgent Army are not recognized. Red Army veterans receive pensions, but as yet in the Ukraine of 2012, the veterans of UPA get nothing. Anatole takes us to see Ivan Lev, an UPA veteran who has a museum in Chernivtsi.

The walls of a large room display portraits of UPA heroes, both men and women. Stepan Bandera's picture has a special place on a corner table, along with a wicker basket of red roses. An erect wooden staff beside the table carries the black and red banner of UPA. And as if to show even more honour to Bandera, more portraits of UPA heroes gaze across from each side of the table and down from above.

"During the war," Ivan says, "our members went out to every village. And after the war they went to Germany. To England. Overseas. Our mission continues on in Ukrainian language schools and summer camps in Canada. United States. Australia."

I have just recently come upon material that Ukrainian historian, Taras Kuzio, wrote on the work of the diaspora:"

On October 16, 2011, members of the 54th branch of CYM "Kershones" Stamford, CT attended a mass and requiem service in honour of the great Ukrainian hero and freedom fighter, Stepan Bandera... Members of the faithful present that day enjoyed a beautiful and emotional homily about the life honour of the great hero on the Ukrainian nation delivered by Reverend Bohdan Danylo, Rector of St. Basil's Seminary in Stamford.

He instructed the children on how they can model their own lives by following his example of self-sacrifice and unwavering dedication to his country. Following the homily, Father Bohdan distributed candles to each child which burned brightly during a stirring execution of the prayer "Vichnaya Pam'yat in honour of the great hero of the Ukrainian nation."

Ivan Lev shows us photographs of a commemoration ceremony for the UPA veterans of the 1944 *Battle of Brody*.

"I was sixteen when I joined the Organization of Ukrainian Nationalists," Ivan says. "1941. Sixty kilometers southwest of Lviv, we fought Germans. A year later, we were fighting in Volynia. Fighting against Germans and Poles."

"And Jews?" I ask.

"Soviet propaganda," Ivan says. "We had Jewish doctors in UPA."

Ivan fought the Red Army in the Battle of Brody. What he doesn't tell me is that this Red Army was made up of the one million Ukrainian troops of the 1st Ukrainian Front Army. Ukrainians against Ukrainians. Ivan was shot in the leg. Captured, he then spent two years of torture in an NKVD prison before being sent to Siberia.

"One square meter of space," Ivan says. "Loud noises and bright lights - twenty-four hours a day. Guards always drunk. Squash my fingers in the iron cage's door. I tell the names only of UPA fighters who are already dead."

Outside the museum, Ivan Lev has built his own personal monument to honour the UPA heroes. A cross is mounted on top of a small hill, a *mohyla*. A blue and yellow flag flaps on one side of the cross, and a black and red flag on the other side. Concrete steps lead up from each side of a plaque of names. Wreaths have been carefully placed. And like everywhere for these monuments in western Ukraine, children from the nearby schools bring flowers.

Later when we're getting into Anatole's van, I open the sliding door for Mavis to get into the back seat. I step up into the front seat, with my left hand hanging on to the open door frame. Anatole has the habit of always opening and closing the doors for us. I had hurried to open the door for Mavis, but Anatole had seen this and he scurried around the back of the car to close her door. It catches my fingers.

"My God! Oh my God!" Anatole says.

"Ivan Lev," I say, and hold up my bleeding fingers. They hurt, but the situation is just too funny to let the pain bother me.

"Drugstore," Anatole says. "We find a drugstore. Get tape, and some salve."

After I get taped up, we drive the several hours it takes to get to Borschiv. By this time, Anatole has quit beating himself over the head for catching my fingers in the car door. He's back on track, trying to convince me of the virtues of UPA, and of the evils of Soviet Russians.

"About Myhailo," he says. "Have you talked to anybody else besides your relatives?"

"We'll go to the museum in Borschiv," I tell him. "Maybe we'll find something there."

We are on the outskirts of Borschiv, eight kilometers from Vovkhivsti.

"There's a hotel somewhere here," I tell Anatole. "I found it on the Internet."

"No," he says. "I have a friend in Borschiv. We're meeting him. He is a friend of the hotel owner. "Better that he takes us. Get a better deal."

The entry to the Shatoshok hotel has two thick logs for gateposts. Each one has the face of a pagan god carved into it. Suspended on these posts is another log with the Shatoshok sign hanging from it. The large courtyard is paved with cobblestones. Gazebos and green shrubs are everywhere, along with old plows, and wagons. The buildings are all made of wood, and the air carries the scent of this wood, and of flowers.

The owner's a retired government official, and he's made this his retirement home. His wife designed the grounds into separate areas, each one representing a different region of Ukraine. Across the way is a twenty hectare apple orchard, nurtured specifically for the smell of its blossoms. The apples, they give away.

For Mavis, our stay here is a welcome surprise. Not only do we have indoor toilet facilities in contrast to Vasyl and Maria's not too clean outhouse but the Shatoshok Hotel has a sauna that is grander than any spa we've ever had the pleasure to bathe in.

Because Anatole is a friend of the owner's friend, the owner charges us only twenty dollars for our room, and ten dollars for Anatole's. Besides that, he invites us, and the director of the Borschiv museum, to have dinner - his gift to have us taste Lemko food, in his Lemko cottage.

"Lemko is a region that's now a part of Poland," Anatole says. "They took it from us."

"My family is Lemko," the owner says.

A young waitress serves a salad of sliced cucumber and tomatoes, and steaming bowls of beet borscht. Cornmeal wraps with cottage cheese and dill. Wraps with cottage cheese and raisins. My favorite filled with poppyseed and honey paste. We eat all of these while sipping delicious coffee. During the meal I ask the museum director if he might be able to find information on Myhailo Warwaruk.

"The Soviet records are likely in the archives in

To Find Myhailo

Ternopil," the director says. "But come to the museum tomorrow. We have Nestor Myzak's book on UPA activities in the Borschiv area."

The museum is Borschiv's most ornate building, built in 1908 as a *Narodni Dim,* a Ukrainian People's Home. It was Borschiv's center for Prosvita. The grandeur of the building is a clear sign of the benevolent Austrian rule of the time.

Anatole spends an hour leafing through Nestor Myzak's book, then decides it would be better if we find the author himself. Nestor Myzak is a history professor at the university in Chernivsti. His home address is in the book.

We meet with Nestor Myzak. He's short and slender, black hair neatly combed, clean white shirt, and dress slacks. We sit at a park table, and I tell him what little I know about Myhailo and Vovkhivsti. He responds with background:

"Austrian rule left a deep and lasting imprint on Halychyna," he says. "When the First World War started, Austria put out a call for soldiers. Thousands of Ukrainians from Halychyna volunteered. More than ten times the numbers the Austrians required."

This causes me to wonder about Canada's internment of Ukrainians during WWI. The Canadian Government tapped onto a rich resource of free labour on the pretense that Canadian Ukrainians might go overseas to fight on the Austrian side. In July of 1914 while visiting in Halychyna, Nykyta Budka, Canada's first Ukrainian Catholic Bishop, wrote back to Winnipeg urging Ukrainian Catholic followers to return home to defend Austria. The bishop feared that Halychyna would be attacked by Russia. A situation not much different than what's talked about today.

That war did take place, and when the Austrians lost, they lost Halychyna. The Russian Empire was collapsing under the weight of a civil war, and to the chagrin of Ukrainian nationalists, the western powers assigned Halychyna to the newly-created nation of Poland. But in halls like Borschiv's Narodni Dim, many of Halychyna's Ukrainians were determined to work for the building of an Independent Ukraine.

Nestor tells about Prosvita, the same youth group that my great-grandfather Danylo started in Vovkhivsti. The name translates as, *to the light.*

"Prosvita had both an educational and military wing," Nestor says. "The latter wing called, *Luhoo,* meaning, *hidden in the bushes."*

In 1925, when Prosvita started up again in Vovkhivsti, a man who was married to Myhailo's wife's cousin, was head of its military wing. His name was Symon Dudka. Prosvita built the village's hall in 1925, helped by the money my great-grandfather sent from Canada.

"Prosvita laid out rules that Ukrainian girls should marry only Ukrainians," Nestor says.

"Young people should not smoke or drink. They should stay out of the Jewish taverns."

Nestor says that when the Soviets took over from Polish Rule in early 1940, they sent young communists, komsomols, to the village halls, encouraging the young people to smoke and drink.

"They took down the icons, and replaced them with pictures of Lenin and Stalin. They brought projector and film to show the joys of collective farm life, encouraging the villagers to form into a *kolkhoz."*

In June, 1940, members of Prosvita in Vovkhivsti destroyed the projector, and beat up on the komsomols. The

To Find Myhailo

next day in retaliation, two hundred NKVD soldiers from Borschiv came to make arrests. One of those arrested was Symon Dudka.

"Were these Russian soldiers?"

"Likely most of them," Nestor says. "Southern Halychyna had over a thousand NKVD. Over half of these were Russian. Just under half were Ukrainian. And then there were some Belorussians, a few Poles, Uzbeks, Armenians, Tatars." He reads the numbers from the statistics listed in his book - "Four Jews."

"How about the komsomol?"

"Stalin sent over seventeen thousand to Halychyna," Nestor says. "Likely Russians. Maybe Jews from Kyiv. Maybe some Ukrainians."

I ask Nestor for reasons of animosity between Ukrainians and Jews.

"Ukrainians were starting into business," Nestor says. "Cooperatives. Their banks and bakeries were taking business away from Jews. And the Prosvita halls were keeping Ukrainians out of Jewish taverns."

"But there's more than that, isn't there," I say, and go on to tell Nestor things he already knows. When the Bolsheviks took power in Russia in the 1920s, they formed the Young Communist League - the Komsomol. Education was a requirement, and few Ukrainians had the opportunity to attend school. Many Jews did. During the early years of the Soviet Union, komsomol cadres were sent far and wide in their attempts to enlighten Ukrainian peasants on the ways, means, and benefits of collective farming. Many of these cadres were Jewish. This plan to collectivize agriculture in the early 30s had some devastating results. Whether it was calculated genocide, or a mix of bureaucratic bungling, political power struggle, and bad weather, one result of collectivization was the starvation of millions of Ukrainians, and it was the komsomol who were Stalin's foot soldiers. In 1940, he tried again - this time in Halychyna.

In Vovkhivsti, aside from episodes like the projector incident, the appearance of the Soviets didn't at first create much alarm. Komsomols came bearing bread and salt, the traditional symbols of greeting. In these first two years, very little collectivization took place. The NKVD deported Poles and wealthier Jews from the Borschiv area, to the *White Bears,* a Ukrainian euphemism for Siberia. Most of the local Ukrainians would not likely have been opposed to this, including those in the nationalist youth group, Prosvita. Up until 1939, the five million Poles in Halychyna owned much of the land. As Poles were removed, the land remained for Ukrainians. But even then, by the end of the two years, most Ukrainians were losing the enthusiasm they may have had for the coming of the Soviets. They were happy to see the Germans.

But the Jews weren't happy to see the Germans. Nestor says nothing about Borschiv's burial pit of two thousand Jews, and he knows nothing about Myhailo's wife, Maria, and her mother helping to hide Sosia Flintenstein and her son in the kerosene storage cave under Solomon's house.

I ask Nestor another question:

"Relatives told me about their cousin," I tell him, "a young girl by the name of Maria Horbova. They said that in 1949, UPA hanged her from a tree by the hall in Vovkhivsti. Do you know anything about that?"

"No. I came across nothing like that," Nestor says. "Not to say that it couldn't have happened. Sometimes an example was made of someone who spied for the special police - the NKVD. Or the NKVD could have done it themselves. They'd make it look as if UPA had hanged her. NKVD would do this to turn the people against UPA."

Nestor's book has information of food requisitions. The Borschiv Soviet in April, 1944, instructed all village heads:

"- Read to the people that the Red Army needs bread! -"

"April was the time when the wheat was needed for seed," Nestor says. "Not to feed the Red Army."

As village head, Myhailo would have had to go door to door. The Germans weren't stupid. They knew enough not to take everything. If a Ukrainian farmer had three cows, they'd take one.

"With the Soviet NKVD," Nestor says, "If the farmer had three cows, he would have to give three cows to the Red Army."

"Our Slavic nature?" I suggest, halfway serious, and Nestor grins.

"The men would be gone from the village, either to the Red Army, or to UPA in the forest. Only mothers, old men, wives, and children, remained in the village."

Nestor says that some of the women served as runners of information back and forth from the village to the UPA bands hidden in the bushes. The runners would have brought the news of the food requisitions.

"In April, 1944, in the Borschiv region," Nestor says, "an UPA leader who was actually a spy for the NKVD, called a meeting in the forest. Five hundred UPA soldiers came with weapons to give to bands from other villages. NKVD soldiers hid waiting, and wiped out the five hundred."

"UPA captured a village head," Nestor says. "When he was questioned, he told UPA the names of ten secret agents of the NKVD."

We visit Symon Dudka's son in Vovkhivsti. We learn that after the Germans retreated in 1944, Myhailo Warwaruk's wife, Maria, suggested to Symon Dudka's wife, that now that the Germans were gone, the Red Army might find and kill Symon. Maria told her that if Symon's band surrendered their arms, perhaps Myhailo could get reassurance from the NKVD for their safety. Symon refused.

Immediately after Myhailo's abduction and disappearance in the summer of 1945, the NKVD located Symon Dudka's band, killing many of the soldiers and sending Symon and his family to Siberia. They were released over twenty years later in 1968, but ordered not to return to their home village. They came home anyway, only to be sent back to Siberia. Seven years later, in 1975, they came home again to stay.

While in Siberia, the Dudkas and other people who had been sent there from the village, wrote letters to Myhailo's widow, stating that it wasn't Symon who had killed her husband. When the Dudkas got back in 1975, Myhailo's widow went to see Symon. He got down on his knees and swore to her that he was not the one responsible for Myhailo's death.

In Vovkhivsti, we go to see Vasyl. I ask him if he remembers anything about the food requisitions.

"I remember hearing something. Father did his best to bypass the homes that housed members of UPA. He'd tell the NKVD official that the house was vacant, even if they both knew it wasn't. It was best for both of them to leave it alone."

"UPA was strong in the village," Vasyl says, "and my father knew them. He talked to them. At Christmas time in 1944, five hundred UPA soldiers with cannons camped on

To Find Myhailo

the hillside by the church. The UPA commander told my father to phone the NKVD in Borschiv to tell them that UPA was waiting to take them on."

They were as strong as ever the following summer when they arrested Myhailo. Shortly after his trial and disappearance, the NKVD came to see Myhailo's wife. They wanted the names of the judges. She knew the names of the three women and two men, but she wouldn't tell. She was afraid of what might happen to her children if she did.

During the three years of German occupation, The Ukrainian Nationalists were organizing into a sizable standing army to fight for the establishment of an Independent Ukraine. UPA's ranks were swelled with Red Army deserters, escaped POWs, previous evaders of conscription into the Red Army, and those hiding out from being taken as slave workers to Germany. The enemies were Red Army partisans on the one hand, and Polish partisans on the other.

But by the middle of 1944, with the Germans gone, and facing a vastly strengthened Red Army and Soviet administration, UPA's tactics had to change. Many of its non-committed members surrendered to NKVD assurances of amnesty and returned to their villages. Some became secret village contacts and suppliers of food for the committed units hidden away in the forests - tiny bands of perhaps ten or twelve members. Others who surrendered became NKVD spies, returning to the forest. From 1944 through to the 1950s, Halychyna was a countryside where in its urban centers, Soviet Power was in place. But at night in the thousands of tiny villages, and in the countless dark hideouts in the Carpathians, it was mostly the Ukrainian Insurgent Army that ruled.

Larry Warwaruk

*Up from the cemetery
a trail leaves the village
of Vovkhivsti
into the thick woods.
An old woman lives alone
A fairy tale Baba Yaga.
Was it on this dark trail
they took Myhailo?*

To Find Myhailo

On our visit to the Dudkas, they told us about an old woman living out in the forest by herself. She at one time had belonged to UPA. We drive out to see her.

Maria Mekoliavna lives alone in a blue-plastered cottage along a forest trail, several kilometers beyond the church and cemetery leading uphill away from Vovkhivsti. Beside the house is an open well, housed in a square of green-painted wood with four posts supporting a roof. Below the roof a rope hangs from a horizontal pole with a hand crank. Beside the well is a white-painted chapel with a green roof topped with a cross.

An ornate plastic fence surrounds the chapel. Inside the chapel, an embroidered red cross centers a white linen altar cloth. Behind the altar stands a statue of Christ. He wears a maroon-coloured robe and his left hand holds a slender wooden cross. On the wall behind hangs a gold-framed painting of Mary and Joseph gazing down at the baby Jesus. Embroidered linen drapes the painting. High up on one side wall, is an icon of Mary, on the other wall, an icon of Christ.

Inside Maria's house, a white linen cloth embroidered with blue and white flowers covers her table.

On the 5th of March, 1945, Maria Mekoliavna jumped in a well. An NKVD soldier pulled her out. Maria, her boyfriend, and eight other men had been hiding in their underground bunker. They were ambushed and all but Maria were killed. Many of the UPA soldiers would kill themselves, rather than be taken alive to be tortured. As for Maria Mekoliavna, she said she'd rather drown in a well than be tortured to tell on others. As an UPA soldier, she had sworn an oath of secrecy.

"Oi, oi," Maria says, "We thought we were safely hidden in our bunker we had dug in the forest. Someone must have informed. The NKVD ambush killed everybody but me."

I look at Anatole, and notice his eyes filling with tears.

"They took me," Maria says, "but along the trail I saw a well. I jumped into it, but then they fished me out. One soldier asked me - why would you want to die?"

As for the torture, she tells us only that they wouldn't give her water. I agree with Anatole that it would be wrong to ask her for any more specifics. But I get him to ask if she knows anything about Maria Horbova being hanged in Vovkhivsti.

"I didn't know her," she says. "I was from a different village."

Maria Mekoliavna's lonely presence hidden, in this forest shelter, is yet another icon of remembrance. Anatole's tears vouch for this.

We make one last visit to Vasyl. I ask him for another possible reason why UPA arrested his father. He said it might have been because Myhailo had considered changing the family's nationality to Polish. In 1945, Stalin arranged that Poles in Soviet Ukraine were to be exchanged for Ukrainians from Soviet Poland. If the family could get to Poland, they might possibly have a chance to get to Canada. I found out later that he changed his religion from Ukrainian Catholic to Roman Catholic, the step it took to become Polish. However - likely due to fear of reprisals - it wasn't long that he switched back to being Ukrainian Catholic. Nationality was of prime importance for UPA. In days of old, when a Ukrainian climbed the economic ladder, it was not uncommon for him to become a Roman Catholic Pole. For a nationalist, this was treason.

Poles did not fare well in WWII Halychyna, but nor did Ukrainians. Nor Jews. During the 1939/41 Soviet Rule, between 800,000 to 1,600,000 people were deported to

To Find Myhailo

Kazakhstan and Siberia. Several hundred thousand of them were Ukrainians, but the majority were Poles, including Jews. This ten to twenty percent of Halychyna's population would have been those who owned substantial amounts of property, including mostly those who were anti-communist nationalists.

Vasyl tells me yet another version of his father's death. In 2009 he told me the story about the well and Myhailo's bones. And during our visit in 2011 Vasyl said that he thought his father had been shot. This time he has another story. I don't know why he didn't tell me this version before. What he tells me, would surely have become big news in the village. I will have to ask other people.

This is what Vasyl says:

"An old woman came to see me. Thirteen years ago. She told me that all these years she kept to her oath of silence - she had sworn, as a faithful member of UPA, to never tell anyone about my father's death. But now as she was approaching her own death, she felt she could no longer remain silent."

"An UPA soldier," the old woman said, "tied a rope to Myhailo's wrists, and dragged him behind a galloping horse."

To Find Myhailo

CHAPTER 5

*Windthorst, Vibank, and Odessa
are villages near my hometown
of Glenavon.
German immigrants settled around these villages.
In my high school days I played football
against their grandsons.
I did not know they were descended from
Katherine the Great's
German Catholic Colonies
on land where now Ukrainians fight
each other.*

Does Myhailo's story involve the Germans? Certainly he administered his village through the three years of German occupation. His Halychyna had experienced two centuries of benevolent Austrian rule that protected Ukrainians from the Poles. Myhailo spoke German fluently, as well as Polish and Russian. Perhaps Ukraine needs a Myhailo to pull it together.

An understanding of Ukraine's history cannot be complete without the knowledge that Halychyna had been in the Austrian Empire, and that the Ukraine of the Russian Empire experienced the agricultural and industrial skills of Mennonite, Catholic, and Lutheran German colonies. These people played a major role in Ukraine's story. And in some ways are attempting to do so again. German Mennonite families from the Outlook area here in Saskatchewan have returned to farm the land of their ancestors. They hire Ukrainians to guard their fields from having their cabbages stolen. At the present time, German money and expertise are busy restoring the 19th century architectural splendor of Lviv. German diplomacy struggles to bring whatever semblance of order it can to the disorder that is Ukraine.

I relate three stories from German acquaintances here in Saskatchewan:

A woman who was a member of the writers' group I belong to, told me a story about Mennonites. She had written several short stories, and we would argue about whether Mennonites came from Russia, or Ukraine. She said *Russia,* and I said *Ukraine.*

Her family's Mennonite colony was on an island in *Zaporegia,* below the rapids of the Dnieper River, a place that was originally the Cossack island fortress - the *Siche.*

To Find Myhailo

"My father was seventeen when he came to Canada with his parents."

In 1922 the family had fled from the Russian Revolution, running from the godless Bolsheviks.

"And the bandits - Nestor Makhno's Black Cossacks. They were even worse than the Bolsheviks."

She told me of an incident where Cossacks swaggered into a relative's house. The family sat at their dinner table, and one of the Cossacks swung his sabre to cut off the father's head. I had heard the same story from her uncle, who was one of the children.

I knew that most of the Mennonites didn't get out of Ukraine in 1922, and they weren't the only Germans who didn't. Mennonites farmed the steppe lands, but colonies of Catholic and Lutheran Germans did too, as did many millions of Ukrainian people.

By 1930 Stalin's collectivization of agriculture was underway. There were two types of collective farms: a state farm - land simply taken from a large landowner, often a Polish Lord. The workers were paid wages. The Mennonite colonies formed into the other type of collective. Each farm family worked its own land of about one hundred and seventy acres, with a share of the crop assigned to the state. Each family could keep one cow and one heifer. When the heifer would have its calf, either the cow or the heifer had to be given up.

Wealthier Mennonite farmers, just like wealthier Ukrainian farmers, were shipped off to Siberia. Many of the more prosperous farmers had already left during the bad times of the Revolution. If those times were bad, worse times were yet ahead. Holodomor, The Hunger, was far worse.

Whether collectivization was Stalin's genocidal plot to kill off all Ukrainians, or simply a bungling tragi-comic bureaucratic mess that led to the starvation of millions; there's no doubt that millions died during 1932/33 that was Holodomor. Quotas, set in the 1931 bumper crop year, were used in a following year of crop failure. Cadres of Komsomol poked sticks in hay stacks, and into the thatched roofs of houses to find hidden bags of grain. They came from Kyiv. To be a member of the Young Communist League you had to be educated. Most Jews lived in towns and cities, and most Jews were educated. In the early 1930s many of the Komsomol were Jews.

    I asked my friend, "Did the Mennonites refer to them as Jews?"

    "Not that I'm aware of," she said. "Just communists, I think. Russians."

    They took everything - even the next year's seed - everything but for the little they didn't find with their probes. Often if a Ukrainian farmer didn't have time to hide his grain, he'd burn it, rather than have a Bolshevik Jew steal it!

    The Mennonites fared better than the Ukrainians. Aid filtered through to them from Germany. Mennonites in Canada and the USA sent money. Soviet bureaucrats opened every letter, from which they took an 11% tax. And the Mennonites always had a cow for milk. If they didn't have grain for the cow, they could feed it pumpkins.

    My friend told me a story about her mother's sister who taught school in her colony, after it was collectivized.

    "Did she have to teach in Russian?"

    "Religion was outlawed, but my aunt could keep teaching in the German language. She was the kindergarten teacher."

    The Russian school inspector came to her class and ordered the teacher to teach the children a new song. He gave

To Find Myhailo

her the words and the tune of a song that praised Lenin. He would return in two months to hear the children sing the song.

"There's no way my aunt would teach the children godless communism, but what could she do? She had an old German book of poems and she found one that praised spring; she could adapt the tune to this poem. Would she dare? It could mean her life, but she would do it regardless. She would put her trust in God."

The children learned the song and they sang it beautifully and enthusiastically. After two months the inspector returned.

"Beautiful singing!" he said. He knew no German, but he was taken by the beauty and enthusiasm of the children's voices.

"To the national competition!" he said. "They have to hear this singing in Kyiv!"

Now what would she do? At the national festival in Kyiv, there would be Party officials attending who would understand German. Life or death, she had no choice but to trust in God.

All expenses paid, the children, parents, and teachers rode the train to Kyiv. Once again, the children sang beautifully and enthusiastically. But would she be arrested?

No. The children's song that was supposed to praise Lenin, but didn't, won first prize! Not one official spoke up about the song's German words in praise of spring.

Back on November the 11th, 1942, My writer friend was a child attending a Remembrance Day service with her father in their Saskatchewan village. As veterans laid wreaths to honour Canadian soldiers slain by Germans in the First World War, the child gazed up at the expression on her father's face. Most everybody would be thinking not only about the *first war*. A *second war* was currently being fought. What was her father thinking? During the Russian Revolution, as a young man barely seventeen, he had gone against Mennonite pacifist belief, to fight for the White Army. After spending weeks in hospital with typhus, he and a cousin found themselves stranded alone in a village the Reds now controlled. They had only the clothes on their backs - their White Army uniforms. Hiding by day, and trying to escape from the village by night, they spotted two Red Army sentries. It was kill, or be killed. These two Mennonite boys killed the Red sentries. To get back to their village, they'd each need a uniform, and the identification papers of a Red Army soldier.

They set out into the countryside, blending in with any Red Army soldiers who were heading in the general direction of their home village. But soon, emaciated from their bout with typhus, they were unable to walk any further. They stumbled upon a Mennonite village.

Family got word of where the boys were - they would have to go with horse and wagon to get them. But the raids of Makhno's Black Cossacks, and the forceful requisitions carried out by the Red Army, had depleted the Mennonite Colony of all the horses and wagons. Makhno had done a job on the grain needed for bread. His Cossacks emptied the sheds and stacked a huge pile of the grain sacks in the centre of the yard. With their sabres they slit all the sacks and the grain spilled on the ground. Makhno invited Ukrainians to help themselves.

The boy's family had two sacks hidden away - enough to grind flour for bread to help carry them through the winter. But now they had to give up one of the sacks to hire a Ukrainian who had a horse and a wagon.

November 11th, 1942, my friend's father had already lived nineteen years in Canada. Nearly a year after this

To Find Myhailo

Remembrance Day ceremony, some of his wife's relatives back in Ukraine loaded wagons with sacks of dried fruit and barrels of salted pork. They were escaping west with the German Army retreat. Three horses pulled each wagon with a cow tethered behind. It took days for the nearly three hundred Mennonites to reach a railway siding, where they boarded seventy per car. Many more Ukrainians were cramming into cattle cars. The train went to Lviv where the people boarded another train that went all the way to Germany. The kindergarten teacher was on that train. This would have been around the time I was born. And the time when soon, Myhailo would once again be Village Representative to the Borschiv Soviet.

    I sit at the kitchen table of a German woman who was nineteen years old when she and her mother got out of East Germany and came to Canada. She describes an event that happened near the end of the war.
    "I was twelve years old," Elsa says. "Our farm was on the Russian front, ninety kilometers east of Berlin. Many refugees from East Prussia were crossing the Oder River to our farm where they'd rest and have something to eat. One day an advance party of twenty Red Army Cossacks showed up. They wore fur hats with a red badge on the front, and a cross. One of them leaned over on his horse and grabbed a child from its mother. The Cossack held the child upside down by the legs. With one swipe of his sabre he cut the child in two. Another Cossack with his sabre plucked a baby from its pram. He flung it high in the air where another Cossack's sabre caught it on the way down."
    Fyodor Dostoyevsky wrote in <u>The Brothers Karamazov</u>:

Turks burn villages, murder, outrage women and children, they nail their prisoners by the ears to fences... cutting the unborn child from the mother's womb, and tossing babies up in the air and catching them on the points of their bayonets before their mother's eyes.

The Cossacks learned from the Turks. What Elsa saw was more of this - a scene at a nearby farm:

"A father, mother, and seven children," Elsa says. "All of them. Their hands and tongues nailed to their dining room table."

Elsa's father was General Otto Graf Von Kummerfeld, a staff general in Berlin. In 1943 he had been party to a failed attempt to assassinate Hitler. Rather than having to be arrested and found guilty, and thus having to forfeit the Kummerfeld family land holdings, her father shot himself.

"He came home from his office in Berlin," Elsa says. "He gave each of our workers a hundred mark cheque. We had a French cook, and the farm hands were Polish. Father then walked into a field of standing rye by the shore of the Oder. We heard a gunshot."

This happened in 1943. A year later the Red Army arrived. In the meantime, Elsa's mother made sure to hide the family's gold, silver, and art treasures. Twelve other landowners did the same.

"In our courtyard, the Cossacks buried my mother up to her neck. They demanded that she tell where the treasures were hidden. They did the same thing with the twelve men, their exposed heads six feet apart. They were left this way for twenty-four hours. No one told. Just before the evening church bells rang, all twelve men were shot in the back of the head. For some reason, my mother was spared."

During the World War I, the Russian tsar exiled Arnold Pehl's German Lutheran grandparents from Volynia,

To Find Myhailo

eastward to Siberia. A few years later during the upheavals of the Russian Revolution, the family returned to their farm.

"My father wanted to go to Canada," Arnold says, "but in 1927 it was no easy task getting out of the Soviet Union."

Arnold's father found enough money to pay a Jew to get him a passport and ship fare, but then he was conscripted into the Red Army Cavalry. He wanted his money back, but the Jew said most of it had been spent.

"So your dad lost the money he paid him?"

"Not really," Arnold says. "The Jew doctored the papers. Dad's younger brother got to go to Canada."

After Arnold's father served his time in the Red Army Cavalry, he fled west across the border to eastern Poland. In the town of Prozorov he found a job laying bricks for a Polish count. He was later married, and in 1936, Arnold was born.

Prorozov was thirteen kilometers from the Bug, a river that in 1939 became the boundary that divided Poland. The count warned Arnold's father that he should pack up his family and flee to the German side. The new Soviet Administration of what was now western Ukraine had already blown up the bridge, but like a band of *Fox Mykytas,* enterprising Ukrainians had planks hidden in the forest. German refugees paid the Ukrainians to lay a pontoon bridge on which they could pass in the dark of night.

"I was three years old," Arnold says, "and I walked the entire thirteen kilometers to the river."

His father and mother carried as much as they could take on their backs. On the plank bridge, his mother showed him that the planks were a darker black than the spaces between - and he was to make sure to step only on the darker spots. Faraway voices carried on the water and Arnold's father wondered if they were the voices of Soviet border guards.

"When we got across the river, my legs were too sore for me to walk. Mom and Grandma took some of the stuff that Dad was packing, and he carried me on his shoulders."

They had no idea where they were going, only that they were heading away from the river. Soon a light appeared from a farm house, and it was there that a Jewish family - a father, mother, two boys, and a girl, took them in for the night.

"The little one cries," the father said. "He must be hungry." He told one of his boys to milk the cow, and then put Arnold on his knees and rubbed his legs. In the morning, the mother prepared food for the Pehls to take with them, and the father gave directions to a station where they could board a train that would take them to Poznan in western Poland.

His father got a job as a building inspector, and his mother worked in a factory assembling radios. In 1943, Arnold's father left Poznan. He had joined the German army. With his knowledge of the Ukrainian language, he became an interpreter for the Secret Service. Four Ukrainian Red Army deserters worked under him. These soldiers would infiltrate back into the Red Army, seeking out other deserters, and reporting military information back to him which he would relay to Berlin. Arnold didn't see his father again until after the war.

"In January of 1945, I was nine years old," Arnold says. He, along with his mother, grandmother, and a year-old baby brother, took the last Warsaw transport train going to Frankfurt-on-Oder. Before Arnold could board the train, his job was to pull dead bodies out of the boxcars, and then he was pulled in through an open window, into a car that was so crowded that his feet never touched the floor. Some men had strapped themselves outside onto ladders, and they froze to death on the way to Frankfurt. The people were all German refugees heading west out of Poland.

"At Frankfurt," Arnold says, "We stayed in a school. I got a birthday cake. The next morning we went to Berlin."

Once they got to Berlin, they were housed in a school beside a big church. The Americans were bombing, and the refugees went into the basement of the school. In the morning, they saw that the church had been flattened, and rubble was everywhere.

Orders were now to get out of the city to the relative safety of the countryside. They took a train to Potsdam where they were able to move in with an old couple who had a sixteen year old Polish boy with them. A few days later, they all left with the old couple's two horses and a wagon.

"We went on a trail in the forest," Arnold says. "And it was raining. I could hear artillery explosions. Branches broke and fell. The horses spooked."

Arnold's mother told the old couple to let the horses go, and she told the Polish boy to start digging a hole for them to spend the night. With broken branches, and a carpet the old couple had brought along, they covered the hole to be sheltered from the rain.

In the morning, they took off walking, knowing only that they had to keep going west. As night fell, they came upon a tin-roofed shed where they spent another night out of the rain. It was that next morning when they found the brick kiln.

"The walls were two metres thick," Arnold says. "Inside were two German soldiers."

They had a machine gun. There was one other German family, and a few released Ukrainian Red Army POWs. German soldiers were hidden in the trees stretching along each side of the kiln, where they formed a line of defense against the advancing Red Army.

The machine gun mowed down wave after wave of attacking Red Army soldiers. A hand grenade was tossed into the kiln, and the soldier who was feeding in the shells, fell on it. The grenade tore open his stomach, and the soldier died on Arnold's mother's lap. His last words were, "Will I ever see my mother?"

"I can still hear him," Arnold says. "The machine gunner then got me to feed the shells. When we ran out of them, he left."

After a while, Red Army soldiers approached the entry. "I was afraid they'd throw in another grenade," Arnold says. "But they didn't. One of them poked his head in and said in Ukrainian, *"Tovarish, dodomo!* (Comrades, go home!)"

Arnold said there were so many Red Army corpses piled up near the entrance that he had to climb over them to join up with a long line of refugees. Several soldiers rode about on horseback, trying to reassure the refugees that they wouldn't be harmed. Arnold's mother who could speak Ukrainian, talked to one of these soldiers, and he got off his horse and told her to ride it and to tell the people they wouldn't be harmed. Arnold's mother also told this soldier that her baby was hungry.

''Find a cow!' the soldier shouted, and sure enough, a cow was found. The wheels of the baby carriage squeaked, and the carriage became very hard to push. Two soldiers took over, and then another one came up with some pork fat to put on the axles. When they got to an open meadow, the soldiers wouldn't let the refugees go any further until the sappers had cleared the road of mines.

"You hear many stories of rape and pillage," Arnold says, "but I can talk only of my family's experience. These Red Army soldiers were kind to us."

To Find Myhailo

The soldier who had spoken to Arnold's mother, introduced her to the Ukrainian who managed a commandeered dairy barn. The manager's name was Nykyta, and he gave Arnold's mother the job of dairy barn boss. When Nykyta got orders to go back east, he introduced Arnold's mother to the unit's head commander. This officer gave her the job of teaching German cooks how to prepare Ukrainian dishes for the soldiers, and later, when the Red Army officers started bringing in their wives and families, Arnold's mother was in charge of the Commanding Officer's household.

By this time, Arnold's father was on the run to get out of the Russian Zone of occupied Germany. Through his work with the German Secret Service, he had already obtained passports, birth certificates, membership cards for the Communist Party, uniforms... anything to suit any situation. Two German soldiers were with him, and his four Ukrainian Red Army deserters. They'd found an abandoned truck, and they siphoned gasoline from abandoned tanks and any other vehicles.

A train sat by an empty station.

"Let's see if we can fire it up," one of the Ukrainians said. They tore wood from the station walls and platform to heat up the engine. They found cases of machine guns and rocket launchers in the station warehouse, and mounted them on a flat car. The railway track ran west into the forest.

Arnold's father was afraid. Red partisans could be anywhere in the forest. The two German soldiers, and two of the Ukrainians, were manning the guns on the flatcar, just in case. All at once, they thought they could hear mortar fire. All four opened up full blast, firing on each side of the train, and lighting up the night sky with tracer bullets. When they got out of the forest, they came upon two German soldiers who asked about all the gun fire. When Arnold's father mentioned partisans, the two soldiers told him there were no partisans in the forest. They'd been cleared out days before. Had they imagined cannon fire? In the dark of night in a black forest, perhaps it is that ghosts can play on the mind.

They left the train, and found a truck, only to be then stopped by a Red Army checkpoint. Now the big test. If found out, Arnold's father and the four Ukrainians deserters could be shot on the spot.

The checkpoint officer took a long time studying the papers. Arnold wondered if the officer could read. German Intelligence didn't miss a trick when it came to forging documents, but one of the two Germans soldiers couldn't speak Russian or Ukrainian. One of the Ukrainians told the officer that his companion spoke only Bulgarian, and they got to go through to the British Zone.

Arnold didn't know the details on how his father and mother kept contact with each other. He remembers something about a Lutheran minister who his mother knew when they were in Poland. He somehow got in touch with her at the dairy farm. He had a letter with him from Arnold's father, saying that he had made it safely to the British Zone.

"Dad risked coming back into the Russian Zone," Arnold says. "He found us, then went back. Mom snuck into the British Zone six times. She hired a woman named Wanda who eventually got us all in. Dad then wrote to his younger brother, who was now farming in Saskatchewan. He sponsored us to get to Canada, but he never did pay back the money Dad had given the Jew for the passport and ship fare."

To Find Myhailo

*From my school days
the War was D-Day.
Normandy. Pearl Harbour.
Hiroshima.
A picture of American soldiers leaning forward
planting a flag on a hill.
I had no picture of the Red army
and nothing of UPA...
But in 1945
Myhailo was in the middle of it all...*

Arnold Pehl said that the Red Army soldiers that he encountered were Ukrainians, and that they were kind to his family. He also said that the Germans were experts at forging passports. In the Ukrainian Diaspora, how many hundreds of names were changed? *Only fools and children tell the truth.* Why end up in Siberia? Or worse yet, with a bullet in the head.

Myhailo's son, Petro, was a Ukrainian Red Army soldier who got his leg shot off during the taking of Berlin. The names on the Red Army Memorial in Vovkhivsti are the names of Ukrainian Red Army soldiers killed by the Germans, and killed in the fight of Ukrainians against Ukrainians. Red Army Memorials like this one are being desecrated throughout western Ukraine. But UPA memorials spring up and priests sprinkle them with holy water.

Countless thousands of Red Army Ukrainian names are etched on memorials throughout eastern and southern Ukraine. The living veterans, widows, and the children and grandchildren of the dead, honour their memory with parades on the 9th of May. But this celebration is being rubbed out in western Ukraine.

Arnold Pehl was one of the many thousands in the diaspora overseas to Canada, Australia, and the USA... He with his family were Germans from Ukraine, and if asked, the Ukrainian Diaspora would be sure to make that distinction. There may have been Poles, Jews, Germans, and Gypsies living in Ukraine, but only Ukrainians are Ukrainians. The ones left behind to fight the Soviets would have agreed to that, and fight they did.

The records kept by the Ukrainian Patriotic Army in the Borschiv area show that in 1945 its units executed two communists, three komsomols, two functionaries, one collective farm manager, six informers, twelve active supporters of the Soviets, and two village heads. Their names are not listed. Though his name isn't mentioned in the written records, Myhailo Warwaruk was one of the two village heads.

By 1945, the Germans were gone from Halychyna, and the Jews mostly exterminated. Stalin ordered that Poles still living in Halychyna be sent west to Poland, traded for Lemko Ukrainians. Soviet Russia became UPA's sole enemy, along with any traitor Ukrainians who supported the Russian occupiers.

Prior to 1945, UPA consisted of its hardcore nationalist ideologues, Red Army deserters and POWs, and Red Army draft evaders. In 1944 when the Soviets returned with their powerful Red Army, they offered amnesty to anyone who would renounce UPA. Most of the POWs, deserters, and draft evaders had previously joined the insurgents simply for their own safety. But now with the Germans gone, and the Red Army's fight turned solely against UPA, the insurgents were no longer as safe as they had been before. Many took up the amnesty offer, and returned to their villages.

Up until this time, the villagers of Halychyna overwhelmingly supported UPA. Their year and a half of Soviet Rule had been more than enough for them. But when the Soviets returned they were far better equipped than they had been in 1939. Besides the amnesty, they opened the Orthodox churches, and the very power of the Red Army convinced many of the villagers that they had no choice but to go along.

As amnesty began getting results, UPA began killing Ukrainians who surrendered. Some of those who did surrender, became informers for the NKVD. UPA killed informers, and their families.

The numbers read, *six informers, twelve supporters of the Soviets*.... Maria Horbova was one of the executed.

In 2007 I had witnessed the youth group camping rally of several hundreds, staged on the hillside of the valley near Lviv. In 2011 I saw smoke bombs defile Lviv's Red Army Memorial. And then in late December 2013, into January and February 2014, the WWII struggles of UPA in its fight for Ukrainian Independence has been reborn at Kyiv's *Maidan*.

To Find Myhailo

*A wall of shields
face-masked men hurling missiles.
Fire everywhere -
hundreds of tires thrown on burning heaps.
A crowd of many thousands -
young and old Ukrainians fill the square.
Snipers from rooftops shoot protestors and police.
Who are these snipers?
For three months the people had demonstrated,
and on February 22nd, pro-Russian President Yanukovych
flees from Kyiv for safety in Russia.*

The UPA veterans who are still alive, and all who are in their graves, are now more than ever, heroes. Negative things said about UPA's activities in the 1940s are regarded as nothing but the lies of Russian propaganda.

The memory of WWII in Ukraine is a dilemma of two opposing narratives. Soviet textbooks espoused the super-human trauma and heroic glory of the Red Army's triumph over the Nazis in the Great Patriotic War. Up to six million Ukrainians, including Myhailo's son, Petro. On the other side, one hundred thousand with OUN/UPA. A comparison unknown in the West. American and Canadian Ukrainian scholars of the Diaspora wrote their version to be taught wherever they could establish Ukrainian Language schools in North America. After 1991, these textbooks were made available for schools in Ukraine, especially in western Ukraine. Monuments to the glory of Stepan Bandera and UPA have been springing up on the landscape as quickly as the giant forms of Red Army granite are disappearing.

To get further into Myhailo's story I have to sift through this paradigm. I have to go back again to Vovkhivsti. Find and talk to Ukrainian families whose names are on its Red Army memorial, if it's still there - *Korchak, Koroluk, Korol, Lozinski, Poroschuk, Rohovski, Sakovski, Solomon, Chevckok, Lazaruk...* and find and talk to families with names on the village's UPA memorial.

But is it safe?

Some time ago in the United States I met a man who is the president of the Minneapolis chapter of Rus, a society whose culture, language, and religion is seemingly identical to Ukrainian. The ancestral homeland of Rus is in the Carpathian Mountains of southwest Ukraine.

"You are Ukrainians?" I asked.

"Not Ukrainian. We are Rus."

"Russian?"

"Not Russian. We are Rus, and not Ukrainian."

For five hundred years the Polish dominated what is now western Ukraine. Orthodox peasants were converted to Catholicism. People hidden in the Carpathians were able to resist, and some of these are known as Rus.

Other ingredients in the soup are Hungarians, Romanians, Slovaks - all can make a claim for parts of Carpathia. And they can be worried about what the new government in Kyiv might do to them. Russian speakers resist Kyiv forces in Donetsk. In the fields of western Ukraine the Germans are back farming. In the cities of Ukraine the Jews are back in business. Polish families might want their land back in Halychyna. The blood-red borscht simmers and ferments. It could explode like gasoline.

I should go once again to Ukraine?

I have a postcard that I bought at an antique store in Rogers, Minnesota. A Polish artist had painted three Hutzul Ukrainian couples seated on a grassy meadow. They are having a Sunday picnic in the Carpathians - on the foothills, where I like to think that an ancestor of mine could well have herded goats. The handwritten script is Polish, but the name of the city is written *Lvov*, which is the Russian spelling. The card's dated the twenty-third of October, 1909, and it's postmarked *Lwow*, the Polish spelling, and also, *Lemberg*, the German name for the city.

Ukrainians bound for Volga, Manitoba, left Vovkhivsti in 1903. They would have travelled north, likely by train from Borschiv to Lviv, to arrive at a newly built and majestic railway station - funded, designed, and built by Jews, Austrian Germans, and Poles. Also built was Lviv's stunningly beautiful Opera House, with six tall pillars out front, and three statues of Greek muses of the arts on its roof. Jews, Austrian officials, and Polish lords and ladies would attend performances, but not Ukrainians.

The buildings that surround the city's central square are those that were built over a hundred years ago. Neither the Nazis nor the Soviets bombed them. Currently the Germans fund restorations. Balustrades have crumbled and balconies collapsed. In 1903 the facades of these buildings would have glistened in the sunlight. But through the fifty years of Soviet neglect, coats of paint and stucco have peeled off. After that, twenty years of Ukrainian independence continued the neglect. It's only been during these last few years that German money has arrived. The Germans are back.

The village my ancestors left behind had the Russian name - *Volkhivsti*. In English it is *Wolf Place*. I talked to a man who farms near Danylo's homestead in Manitoba. This man's grandfather also came from Volkhivsti. I asked this farmer if he knew the Ukrainian word for wolf, and he said *wowkh*, which is most certainly Polish, and not Ukrainian. The Volkhivsti Ukrainians who emigrated in 1903 came to Canada with many Polish words. Nine years before this, my great-grandfather, Danylo, one of the founders of Volkhivsti's Prosvita, saw his mission as one to educate his people that they were not Poles. Did Danylo know he was Ukrainian? At least did he know there was a clear separation between Ukrainian and Russian? I'm not entirely sure, because nine years after the families from Volkhivsti arrived at their plots of land along the south shore of Lake Winnipegosis, they built their school and called it *Don*, a famous Russian river. They soon had their store and post office named *Volga*, another Russian river. In 1932 they built their hall and named it *Don*. At least, it would seem, they didn't hate the Russians.

To Find Myhailo

In my university days, I had a keen interest in Russian history, but not, Ukrainian. However, as my life enters its eighth decade, I now feel I am Ukrainian. As a youth, I was completely assimilated into the English Canadian culture. But now, like many of the third generation, I seek my Ukrainian roots. But in so doing, I find myself in a troubling dilemma. Our mainstream media reports that the Stalin-like Vladimir Putin has ordered the Russian Army into Ukraine. An evil dictatorship has invaded a freedom-loving pro-western democracy. My perceptions stare in opposition to this seemingly unanimous Ukrainian Canadian voice expressed by the children of the Diaspora. Even our Prime Ministers speak out for Kyiv. Stephen Harper had said that the international community stands against Pro-Russian Terrorists in Eastern Ukraine. He called the Russians *imperialist aggressors*. Justin Trudeau, though milder, spouts the same talk.

But my lonely thoughts tell me that a fringe element of western Ukrainian fascists were the killing snipers at Maidan, that they were the arsonists who burnt the Pro-Russian Ukrainians they had locked in the Odessa Union Hall, and that they were the force that downed the Malaysian airplane - all of this in collusion with the American CIA and hired Blackwater mercenaries.

Am I a fool for Soviet/Russian propaganda? Whatever I am, I hope only that matters settle. I hope I can go back to the village to ask as many questions to as many people as I can. I want to get as much as l can of Myhailo's story. From what I can tell so far, he stood in the middle, between West and East, something that appears impossible today, and as it turned out for Myhailo, impossible for him.

While the vast steppes to the east had been under Russian Rule for several centuries, the Austrian Empire and Poland ruled *Halychyna,* merely 10% of Ukraine's total land mass. Halychyna's Ukrainians came face to face with Russians only after 1939.

At the end of the war when the Germans were driven out of Ukraine, many UPA insurgents fled with them, but several thousand retreated into the Carpathian Mountains to continue the fight against the hated Soviet government.

On two of our visits to western Ukraine, Anatole, our guide/translator/friend took us on the visits to Ivan Lev, the UPA veteran who had his own personal OUN/UPA museum in Chernivsti. He had been in the Galician Division *(Halychyna)* and had fought and was captured during the Battle of Brody. He was then interrogated/tortured for two years, then sent to Siberia where he met his future wife. He told me that the Ukrainian prisoners built and lived in far nicer houses than did the Russian prisoners.

He said that after the war, OUN's organization spread throughout the world and remains active to the present day. He said also that they have youth organizations in nearly all the high schools in western Ukraine, and that they hold outdoor camps throughout the year and during the summer. Anatole said that his son attended these camps. Natalya, who is Anatole's counterpart for us in Lviv, told me that her younger brother attended these camps, and that he was one of the demonstrators at the 2011 Victory Day demonstration that Mavis and I observed.

That evening during our first trip in 2007 where we attended the weekend youth rally in the valley on the outskirts of Lviv, the black and red flags of Stepan Bandera were everywhere on the hillside along with tents and the blue and yellow flags of a reborn Ukraine. A large movie

To Find Myhailo

screen showed outdoor war games the youth camps performed during the year. It seems that the younger generation in western Ukraine are well trained and OUN inspired to be totally anti-Russian and determined to erase any memory of the Red Army heroics during the war. But can it also be that in the large area of Ukraine, the memory of the Red Army heroics of the forefathers are cherished, but guarded due to the current political situation?

By April of 1944, the Germans were gone from Vovkhivsti, and Myhailo once again represented the village at the reinstated Borschiv Soviet. The war, both for the local Soviet, and for the local Ukrainian nationalists, was now exclusively a fight between themselves, like in every other region of Halychyna. And if nominally the Soviets were in control, this was not the case in the village. It was Christmas, 1944, when five hundred heavily armed UPA insurgents camped on a hillside by the Ukrainian Catholic Church - not far from Myhailo's house. The commander phoned Myhailo to tell him to phone the NKVD in Borschiv and tell them to come to Vovkhivsti if they wanted a fight. UPA would be waiting for them. I'm curious to know if this commander was Symon Dudka. Whatever the case, at this time Myhailo communicated with both sides. He in fact billeted and fed some of the five hundred insurgents. I hope to find out how long he remained on speaking terms with UPA, because ten weeks after Easter in 1945, they arrested him. Following his death, UPA's battle against the Soviets continued on for at least ten more years. For the next sixty years, the memory steeped. Embers smoldered. And today the flame rekindles. For a Ukrainian nationalist, the terms *Soviet* and *Russian* are synonymous, as are *Putin* and *Stalin*.

Larry Warwaruk

If Myhailo Warwaruk were alive today, what role would he take in today's Ukraine? From what I've learned about him so far, it does seem that he tried to play to all sides. Who could ever do that, and succeed, in today's Ukraine? Throughout the war, he played a prominent role in the village, and also before the war. He took the role of a politician in February of 1940 when the Soviets came to Vovkhivsti.

Before the war, this homeland of my ancestors had been under Polish Rule. Myhailo's home was adjacent to a Polish dairy farm at the northwest corner of the village. Myhailo was foreman, and in charge of the farm's four horses. He spoke four languages: Polish, German, Russian, and his native Ukrainian. Forty-six years earlier, his uncle, Danylo, had been one of the founders of the village's Ukrainian youth group, *Prosvita*. In 1903 Danylo emigrated to Canada, but he didn't forget what he had started. In his new country of Canada it would take much time and much hard work to raise enough money just to survive, let alone anything extra to send back to Vovkhivsti. But he did it - in 1925 Danylo sent the money for the building of Vovkhivsti's *Prosvita* hall. During Polish Rule, Danylo's nephew, Myhailo, had successfully lobbied with the local Polish governance to keep the Ukrainian school open. Because he was the farm manager, both Poles and Ukrainians respected his leadership skills. He could make Poles and Ukrainians work together. This same ability soon helped him work with the Russian and Ukrainian Soviet functionaries, and then later with their enemies, the Germans.

Myhailo was connected to the Polish community, the Jewish community, the Ukrainian insurgents, and he had been the foreman over all the Ukrainian workers who had been employed at the Polish dairy farm. Myhailo was chosen now as village head, and village representative to the Borschiv Soviet.

To Find Myhailo

In the late fall of 1941, the Germans arrived. Anything had to be better than the year and a half of Soviet economics with its experimental bungling, and the village held a generally pleasant memory of former Austrian German Rule. The villagers welcomed the *Wehrmacht,* and the Germans saw that they could leave Myhailo's local administration in place. Meanwhile Symon Dudka, freed from a Soviet prison, could once again organize in the forest.

Myhailo had used his influence to keep his oldest son, Ivan, from being conscripted into the Red Army, and now he protected his second son, Petro, from being sent to work in Germany, and during the first four months of 1944 when the Germans were rounding up Jews, his wife and her mother helped hide Sosia Flintenstein and her son in the cave on the southern outskirts of Vovkhivsti, the cave that had at one time been a Jewish merchant's storehouse for barrels of kerosene. When the Germans took over, the farmers hoped that their cows would be released. This didn't happen however, so they simply stole them back. Soviet school teachers had been mandated to turn their students against religion. Children were told to inform on their parents - a reason enough to welcome the Germans.

In 1942, my father, who at first had been a school teacher in Manitoba, bought a grocery store in Saskatchewan, and his connection to the war was to be on the Wartime Prices and Trade Board which involved Canada's contribution to the war effort. I don't think Ukrainian Canadians at that time knew anything at all about what was happening in Ukraine. Right after the war, many more Ukrainians arrived in Canada, and the stories they brought were all about the evils of Stalin and Communism. Some might have experienced *Holodomor,* but most of them came from western

Ukraine - the areas that hadn't belonged to the Soviet Union before the war. But they knew of many friends packed into railway cars and shipped east to perish in Stalin's gulags, or simply to be shot. As for their own involvement in the war and the story of UPA, this post-war Diaspora remained mostly silent about the fate of Jews and Poles and Ukrainian Red Army supporters in villages like Vovkhivsti.

In my search for Myhailo, I see characteristics of myself that I think are genetic. In my childhood, though I achieved top grades in school, nearly every report card had teacher comments that Larry is messy, he speaks out of turn, he has no respect for rules. I see these characteristics in Ukraine. Our guide, Anatole, coined a name for himself - *No Rules*. Ukraine is a country of no rules. Do whatever works. I think of Ivan Franko's, Mykyta. The fox outwits the wolf and the bear. Mykyta cares only for his own survival and his family's. Fox Mykyta is a Ukrainian anarchist.

During the last week of November in 2014, Mavis and I fly to Cuba for a sunshine holiday. While there, I meet up with a group of vacationing Ukrainian immigrants from Toronto. A young man from Kyiv is with them. He'd been on a fund-raising mission to Canada and he tells me that he got a nice Remington rifle for himself.

"What's happening in Ukraine?" I ask.

"I fight in the Donbas," he says. "At the front. With the Donbas voluntary battalion. And again at Mariupol with the Azov voluntary battalion."

"Whose side do the people support?"

"Sometimes one way, sometimes another. They're miners. Hard on their brains from the dust in the coal mines. Can't think for themselves. Always drunk."

"What do you think about Poroshenko?"

To Find Myhailo

"Not much. The regular army is improving, but the voluntary battalions are in control."

He tells me that most of the soldiers in the voluntary battalions had been members of *PLAST* - the Ukrainian boy scouts formed in Lviv in 1911, and named after the *plastun*, the historical name for Cossack scouts. The soldiers in the voluntary battalions are the same young men that Mavis and I saw demonstrating on Victory Day in Lviv. The same young people we saw in military training on the big screen above the stage at the youth campout in the valley near Lviv. The same blackshirts at Maidan.

Anatole had told me that the regular army was useless. He said that the future was with *PLAST*. The UPA veteran, Ivan Lev in his museum in Chernivsti, told me that UPA had never died. That *PLAST* organizations existed overseas - in Canada, The USA, Australia - organizations for the Diaspora's youth. With the fall of the Soviet Union, the youth groups of UPA once again formed to thrive in Ukraine.

The young man from Kyiv says he is going back to fight. He'll go once again with the Azov voluntary battalion where he will be in charge of 300 men. He says that at Mariupol, one of his friends was shot in the head. Another went mad.

Pro-Russian media show videos of unarmed civilians being shot at Mariupol. Pro-Kyiv media show videos to dismiss this accusation as simply an example of clever KGB inspired Russian propaganda. I ask the Azov commander if he can predict what will happen in Ukraine.

"Not for me to predict," he says. "I simply carry out my patriotic duty to fight."

Canada sent two hundred troops to train Ukrainian soldiers. Our troops train only the regular Army soldiers, and not members of volunteer nazi battalions like Azov.

Larry Warwaruk

Did Canada know that an Azov commander had already obtained a fair share of Canadian arms and money?

The fight rages on. Though I'm one hundred years removed, I feel Ukraine's horror. In my youth I knew that my grandparents came from Ukraine, but I didn't know that their Ukrainian land they had left behind was part of the Austrian Empire. I didn't know that after WWI, this land became Poland again, as it had been for 500 years ruled by a Polish/Lithuanian Empire.

I didn't know that in 1922, Lenin decreed that the Ukrainian lands of the Russian Empire, be recognized as Ukraine, and that Ukrainian language schools be established. I didn't know that he gave the Donbas to Ukraine so that its industrial workers could spread the word of communism to the private-enterprising Ukrainians. The 1920s saw a rapid rise of a Ukrainian identity separate from the Russian. In 1939 Stalin added eastern Poland to Ukraine, the land of my grandparents.

But 1933 brought Holodomor. Ukrainians rebelled against Stalin's collectivization of agriculture. The rebellion failed, and millions of Ukrainians starved to death. Collectivization endured, and the remaining Ukrainian families and the imported Russians who worked these farms would later be in the forefront to fight the Nazi invasion. The Red Army conscripted Ukrainians numbering in the millions. Many were killed. Many were captured. Many deserted to fight for the other side. But many more thousands continued fighting in the Red Army's prolonged struggle, on to the 9th of May, 1945. Victory Day. Myhailo's son, Petro, took part in the final advance. It is this drive that many Ukrainians want to remember.

But many want the memory erased.

To Find Myhailo

In 1941 it took only a few months for Operation Barbarossa to reach the outskirts of Moscow, just these few months to sweep almost unhindered across the broad stretch of Ukraine. But then the Russian fronts at Stalingrad, Moscow, and Leningrad dug in. During these first few months, thousands and into the millions of poorly equipped Ukrainian Red Army soldiers had been surrendering, if their Russian officers hadn't managed to shoot them in the back. These soldiers in the autumn of 1941 had more than sufficient reason not to want to fight for Russian Soviets who had previously inflicted *Holodomor*. Many from *Halychyna* who surrendered were those who hadn't managed to evade conscription. Many of their fathers could well have fought on the Austrian German side during WWI.

Petro Warwaruk's situation was far different. During the period when the Red Army conscripted the million or so Ukrainian soldiers who later deserted or surrendered, Petro's older brother hid in the forest to keep from being conscripted. During the German occupation, Myhailo used his influence to keep both Ivan and Petro from being shipped west to the German workforce.

After April of 1944, when the Germans retreated, the increasingly successful Red Army conscripted 18 year-old Petro. His memory, and that of the thousands and thousands of new conscripts, would however, be one of victory.

But their success with the fall of Berlin did not end the Red Army's fight. UPA units, many made up of those who surrendered or deserted in autumn 1941, had been on the German side. Most of their fight during the German occupation had been to clear their Ukrainian lands of Poles and Jews. With the Germans gone, and with the Poles and Jews gone, the fight was now totally against the Russian Soviets, and those that supported them, including fellow UPA soldiers who had turned in their arms on promises of amnesty when they realized they no longer had German support. Thousands had fled west, to eventually reorganize in far off places like Canada, Australia, and the USA. The struggle is far from over.

To Find Myhailo

CHAPTER 6

Dragged behind a horse.
Thrown down a well.
Hanged from a tree.
A Cossack skill to fasten
a girl's legs to tied-down saplings,
one on each side of her,
and then to cut the ropes...
In May of 2014 the Odessa union hall
was locked from the outside, set afire,
and mangled bodies burned...
In front of the hall Fox Mykyta circles...
Here it is, the dark side...
He snarls and snaps. He has them squeaking,
barking, howling, quacking, singing songs
and flying banners...
The Union hall?
All Russian lies.

The volunteer battalions lead the way to cleanse east Ukraine of Russians. *Sovoks* are sub-humans who support Soviet Communism. They worship Lenin statues. Sovoks speak Russian. The Azov commander I talked to in Cuba told me that Sovoks are dimwitted miners whose brains are clouded with coal dust.

Our media identifies Putin as the instigator and power behind Sovok treason, and that Ukraine's struggle for democracy is a battle against the invasion of Russian army soldiers and tanks. Ukraine needs help from the Free World. The fight is one of freedom vs. slavery. *Svoboda* means *freedom*. The party is strong in Lviv and throughout *Halychyna*. Bandera is the hero. *Slava Ukraina, Slava Heroem - Glory to Ukraine - Glory to the Heroes* - the Bandera greeting and response that's sounded everywhere today in western Ukraine.

Activists like the Azov commander attend Ukrainian Canadian Congress events where they receive donations of money and weapons to take back to Kyiv. The Azov Battalion played a leading role in the Odessa Union Hall massacre of *Sovoks*. Prior to the 2nd of May, 2014, these people may have been willing to come to some agreement with the government in Kyiv, but not after the massacre. These people will never forget.

Over 40 were killed. Some say it could have been as high as 300. Most of the people, especially children and women, were hacked with axes and clubbed to death with wooden sticks in the basement of the Trade Unions House. *Sovoks* were locked in, shot, burned, gassed, garroted, beaten with bats and chains, and raped. A man who had managed to get out of the hall, said that even before the smoke had spread inside, he saw people leaning outside windows trying to take a breath of fresh air. The New York Times reported that:

> As the building burned, Ukrainian activists sang the Ukrainian national anthem, witnesses on both sides said. They also hurled a new taunt: "Colorado" for the Colorado potato beetle, striped orange and black like the pro-Russian ribbons. Those outside chanted "burn Colorado, burn," witnesses said. Swastika-like symbols were spray painted on the building, along with graffiti reading "Galician SS," though it was unclear when it had appeared, or who had painted it.

God forbid this be reported to our Canadian Parliament.

Most of the participants in the chanting crowd were not from Odessa. Fans had come from Karkhiv to watch their team play football against Odessa. Included were busloads of volunteer battalions with a plan to wipe out pro-Russian activists camped in tents near Odessa's Trade Unions Building.

On May 3rd *The Moscow Exile* reported that:

> Ukraine clashes: dozens dead after Odessa building fire.
>
> The Trade Union building was set alight after a day of street battles in the Black Sea resort city.

From *The Guardian*, May 5th:

> The burials were the first of dozens that were to take place over the next few weeks:
>
> Marken, 44, was a key supporter of a semi-permanent protest camp in Odessa against the current Kyiv government that was burned to the ground on Friday before fighting moved to the nearby trade union building. At some point during the melee he was badly beaten and died in intensive care in a local hospital the following day.

The other funeral was Maksim Nikitenko, 31, who was also killed early on during the struggle inside the trade union building. "They fought and cracked open his skull and then he was thrown out the window," said Petya, a friend.

Nikitenko was not a separatist or an extremist, but he ran to defend the trade union building when he heard it was under attack, Petya added.

Before the burials Marken's open casket lay in the local parliament building for friends, colleagues and residents of Odessa to pay their last respects.

Outside an angry crowd gathered and the regional governor, who had come to lay flowers, was assaulted and forced to flee ignominiously down the corridor. When pallbearers carried the coffin out of the building people clapped and chanted "Odessa is a Russian city", "Hero, hero, hero!" and "Odessa will not forgive nor forget."

The tents on the square were set on fire. The pro-Russian activists then sought refuge in the Trade Unions House, only to be trapped. Once inside, they were attacked by Right Sector thugs who were already in the building. This way it was possible for Right Sector to kill the *Vostoks* with impunity, with great relish, and without witnesses. *Vostoks* were burned through to their bones. Firefighters appeared only after the massive entrance doors were burned through.

Pictures show charred bodies on the ground floor near the entrance doors. But there are also pictures of charred bodies on the higher floors where there was no open fire. There's a picture of a barricade of tables, chairs, and cabinets not touched by fire, yet charred bodies lie nearby. The barricade prevented the *Vostok* from fleeing to the higher floors.

To Find Myhailo

One picture shows a female corpse dragged across the floor space from somewhere else in the building. Who dragged her, and why? Some of the dead people have burnt heads and shoulders only. Clothing below their chests was not affected by fire. Somebody had poured something flammable onto the upper bodies to set them ablaze. Some bodies had their hands and wrists burnt.

A strange whitewash can be seen on the floor. Is this an extinguisher powder the punishers used in order to not burn themselves? A dead young man and woman are not burned or garroted, but their necks are broken. The badly burnt corpse of a woman lies near the elevator. She is naked below the waist. Raped?

There is a picture of a woman on the third floor of the building. Someone had garroted her with a wire. She's bent over backwards against a desk, her belly stretched upward to point at the ceiling, her head fastened down to the desktop.

A dark foreboding monument....

Larry Warwaruk

I'm drawn to the Warwaruk
home in Vovkhivsti as it was
200 years ago
long before Myhailo.
The house still stands not far from
the Ukrainian church on a hill.
Further down, on the main street
the Polish church
of more than 200 years ago
is no longer there.
West of the cemetery is
a road into the forest dark and musty
where mushrooms grow...
And today, somewhere
far into the deep dark trail...
Myhailo's bones...?

To Find Myhailo

At least as far back as 1820, Warwaruks have been living in the same place in Vovkhivsti. Documents from that date show a Hryhori Warwaruk as owner of seven plots, comprising a total land area of four hectares. Hryhori was Danylo and Fedor's grandfather. It appears that throughout the 19th century, and right through to WWII, from their adjacent seven plots of land, the Warwaruks were in charge of managing a Polish estate much larger than their four hectares. During the 1930s when Myhailo was the estate's farm boss, the Polish landowner, Vadas Mishterevych, lived in far away Lviv. One of Myhailo's duties was to see to the operation of a *kirat* - a horse-powered device used to chop grass and straw to feed the livestock.

After the Germans retreated in 1944, the process to collectivize the Mishterevych land came into play. As farm manager, Myhailo had been in charge of all the equipment, and then as the village representative to the Soviet, it became his responsibility to turn all the tools over to the *kolkhoz*. People tried to take things, but Myhailo would not allow it. A woman, Anna Melnyk tried to take the *kirat*, but Myhailo stopped her. She then complained to the local UPA that Myhailo supported Soviet power, and not the people. This helped to turn some of the locals against Myhailo. The community was split: either you went along with collectivization, or you supported UPA. It appears that the Warwaruks went along.

There were two Petros connected to Myhailo - his oldest son Petro who I interviewed, and a brother Petro who died in the war. In 1944, The Red Army conscripted him, and in the following year on the 21st of April, the brother Petro was killed in battle and is supposedly buried in Germany somewhere east of Berlin. His name is etched on the Red Army Memorial in Vovkhivsti, as is Myhailo's.

Larry Warwaruk

And in 1949, as the Ukrainian Insurgent army continued on in its desperate struggle against the Soviets, Maria Horbova, who was Myhailo's 19 year-old niece, was hanged from a tree. Her name is also etched on the Red Army War Memorial in Vovkhivsti, if the monument hasn't already been demolished. This could happen, for the government in Kyiv passed a law that bans the display of Soviet communist symbols, including ribbons, medals, flags, and monuments.

These Soviet symbols were many, and in their style of socialist realism, they were gigantically grandiose. On Kyiv's *Lavra* riverbank, the *Motherland* Statue reaches 102 metres to the sky. Her right hand holds a blunted sword, its tip sawed off after Ukraine's 1991 Independence. On the day before Russia's Victory Day celebrations, this May of 2015, poppies crowned the statue's brow. There are no orange and black ribbons, but instead, a ribbon of blue and yellow complements the poppy tiara on The *Motherland's* brow. But yet her left hand still bears a shield marked with the Soviet hammer and sickle. What will be *Motherland's* fate? Will she topple like Lenin statues? Since the pro-Western government swept into power, the toppling of these statues has been so common that they've taken the name, *Leninopad,* or *Lenin-fall.* Over five hundred of these have already toppled, but no one yet knows what to do with the Soviet-era *Motherland.* Her arms extend east towards Russia. On the Dnieper riverbank to the south of the *Lavra* - the cluster of churches and hermit caves - the old Soviet *Motherland* still stands as the wartime defender of Kyiv.

I draw a fantasy. On her shield, the Ukrainian trident replaces the Soviet hammer and sickle. She stands on the roof of a Red Army museum. Replace the Soviet contents of the museum with the artifacts of UPA. There is a precedent. During the war, the town of Kosiv in Halychyna

To Find Myhailo

was predominantly Jewish. Nearly all were killed, and the rabbi's mansion has been turned into a museum. There are two parts; one depicts the heritage of Hutzul culture in Carpathia. The other part shows UPA's patriotic struggle for Ukraine's independence, with of course no mention of what UPA did to the Jews.

What better display could there be for Ukraine's Independence, than to convert a Red Army museum into a showpiece for the artifacts of UPA? And on its roof, *Motherland* stands. Why not extend her sword back to its original length, this time to fight the Russians.

Ivan Franko's statue on his grave in Lviv's cemetery poses a problem perhaps not as easy to solve as *Motherland*. There's no doubt that the bare-chested Franko wielding a pick-axe is as pure a model as there can be of Stalinist socialist realism. To dress a Ukrainian Nationalist literary hero in Soviet Socialist garb is a flat-out contradiction. Will the headstone of Ivan Franko, the creator of *Fox Mykyta*, have to be destroyed?

But whether *Soviet,* or *Nationalist,* the monuments of Ukraine's heroes show an art form broad and bold. Stepan Bandera's monument in Lviv stands taller than any Lenin. A monument sends a message. In the Warwaruk story, Maria Horbova hangs from a tree. This was meant to send a message. The reading hall in Vovkhivsti no longer exists, and the bronze plaque that honoured my great-grandfather's financial contribution, sent from Manitoba to help build this hall, has been a long time lost. In 1949 UPA hanged Maria Horbova from a tree beside this hall. There is much I want to know about her. How was she related to Myhailo? Did her hangmen pin a sign to her breast, as a warning to other girls to stay away from Red Army soldiers? If I go once again to the village and ask old people these questions, will I be subject to the new law that forbids negative comment about UPA? The maximum penalty is ten years in jail.

Safe for me to go? The Russian side in the social media tells me that a prominent pro-Russian editor in Kyiv, Oles Buzyna, on April 16/2015, was fatally shot outside his home. A lawmaker from Kyiv's parliament named Boris Filatov told colleagues, "One more piece of shit has been eliminated." From another named Irina Farion: "This death will neutralize the dirt this shit has spilled. Such people go to history's sewers."

According to the Russian bias, Kyiv's parliament is not a kindly place, and further to such comments, trendy art exhibitions tell the same story. In April 2014 an exhibition in the Modern Art Centre in Kyiv featured the exhibition *Beware of Russians*. Actors sporting St. George ribbons were placed in zoo cages with *Do not feed* signs. The *Russians* were drinking vodka, playing balalaikas, honouring Putin, and threatening visitors. In Kharkiv the exposition *Goddess of War* featured images titled *Dogs of the DPR,* showing dead bodies of Donbas defense forces. One week after the *Beware of Russians* exhibition, pro-Russian activists were burned alive in the Odessa Trade-Union House.

At this point I'm more confused than ever. Is all of this the slick ploys of Putin's KGB propaganda, stemming from the seeds that Stalin planted years ago? My perceptions are rooted in the witnessing of the 2011 Victory Day demonstrations in Lviv. I was there. Young men wearing red/black masks, ripped Cross of St. George Medals off the lapels of Red Army Veterans. I see the current fight in Ukraine as a contest over who will be Ukraine's heroes: the veterans and deceased of Bandera's UPA who fought the Soviets, or the Red Army Ukrainians who fought and defeated Nazi Germany?

To Find Myhailo

Born in 1943 Canada,
Spoiled
The War only made us rich
Old enough in the 50s
To watch the movies...
Raise the flag on Iwo Jima
Come, we have it all...

Larry Warwaruk

After the fall of the USSR, a new generation is schooled in Ukraine. It wants to be like us. Wants the things it thinks the West has. Wants democracy. Sofiya is of this new generation. She is the guide and translator who showed us the caves under the banks of Kyiv's Dnieper River. This 2015 summer she sings at Ukrainian Festivals in Alberta, raising money for the Ukrainian Army. During the 2004 Orange Revolution in Kyiv's Independence Square, she and her mother stuffed flowers into the rifle barrels of Yanukovich's militia. While she's here I should get in touch with her, but she's at the forefront of the very hype I'm questioning.

The Ukrainian Canadian organizations that fund her tour might not look kindly on the image I'm trying to paint of Myhailo, might not look kindly on someone writing in support of a Ukrainian who was a village representative to a Soviet. They might not want to hear about his fate, or the fate of Maria Horbova. No talk today of the Odessa massacre. No talk of who really were the snipers at Maidan. Nothing on the downing of the Malaysian airplane. Blame Putin. Enough said. Canada supports Ukraine's fight for independence. Putin is a Hitler and a Stalin. Saskatchewan shows support for Ukraine. The starving Holodomor girl stands forlorn on the grounds of our legislative building. *Slava Ukraina, Slava Heroim.*

Sofiya has brought hundreds of military dog-tags for sale. They show the *Trident* - with some of the tags painted yellow and blue, and others the black and red of Bandera - *Slava Heroim UPA.* Inscribed on the back of each dog-tag is the phrase, *I support Ukraine.* They sell for $20.

Ukraine has a vengeful heritage, nowhere more graphically depicted than in Nikolay Gogol's 1842 novella, *Taras Bulba.* In this story, atrocities abound, and they seem glorified in a dressing of proud savagery, as if these war-

To Find Myhailo

ring deeds are badges of honour. - An honour that shows the dark side:

> *Taras made raids all over Poland, burned eighteen towns and nearly forty churches... "Spare nothing," was the order of Taras. The Cossacks spared not the black-browed gentlewomen, the brilliant, white-bosomed maidens: these could not save themselves even at the altar, for Taras burned them with the altar itself. Snowy hands were raised to heaven from amid fiery flames, with piteous shrieks, which would have moved the damp earth itself to pity and caused the steppe-grass to bend with compassion at their fate. But the cruel Cossacks paid no heed; and, raising the children in the streets upon the points of their lances, they cast them also into the flames.*

I think of the fire in the Odessa Union Hall. Putin KGB Photo-shopped depictions? The picture of the garroted woman, bent over backwards against a desk. Grotesquely arched. The back of her head fastened to the desk.

Many of Sofiya's generation would call this picture a lie of Russian propaganda, or else they'd ignore it completely. Their school years since 1991 have drilled them on the horrors of Russian imperialism - Stalin and his bolsheviks, famine and state repression in the 1930s, KGB and Putin. Down with Red Army statues. Up with Bandera. *Slava Ukraina, Slava Heroim.*

I think of Myhailo, and Maria Horbova...

Larry Warwaruk

*For Canadians, the war in Europe
is over in 1945
The Western Front.
No one has heard of an Eastern Front.
In summer of 1946, returned pilots
take people for rides.
One airplane comes to Glenavon...
I'm three years old
Shorty Osborne lives next door -
He's an old man, and my special friend.
Sometimes when I don't like
what Mother has for dinner
I go to Shorty's for pork sausages and creamed corn.
On the day the airplane arrives
Shorty takes me to the sports ground
and treats me to an airplane ride
without my mother knowing...
I have a faint memory of this childhood vision
of the fields and the village
seen from high up in the sky...
In this same summer of 1946 there is famine
in Vovkhivsti.
Is Myhailo still held captive in the forest
or is he already dead?
In 1946 Maria Horbova is 16 years old
Does she already have her Red Army boyfriend?
What's Ukraine's real story?
Ask Fox Mykyta and he will say that
Only Fools and Children Tell the Truth.*

To Find Myhailo

I have a 1920 edition of the book, *Fox Mykyta,* published in Jersey City, USA. The text is Ukrainian, translated from the story Ivan Franko wrote in German - at least so it says in this edition. In my struggle with the Ukrainian script, lines speak out to me that tell of life in Halychyna around the time my grandparents left:

It was spring. King Lion Tsar Lev, ruler of all the beasts, stood on the terrace of his palace and admired the beauty of the rolling countryside that stretched away in the far distance.

Tsar Lev would be the Austrian governor, residing in the city of the Polish nobility and Jewish money-lenders - the City of Lviv, which at that time was *Lemberg,* or the Polish *Lwow.*

His subjects were not angels, but creatures of different races.

Everyone obeyed the king's command. All except one, that is. Lys Mykyta Haidamaka:

Nothing better represents the spirit of Ukrainian Independence than do the Haidamaki Cossacks. Because of the massacres of Jews, Jesuit priests, Greek Catholic Ukrainians, and Polish nobility, the term *Haidamaki* in the Polish language became a pejorative label for all Ukrainians. But not pejorative in the oral traditions of Ukrainian folklore, and not for Taras Shevchenko. His poetry can be said to immortalize the Ukrainian Cossack as a major part of the heart of Ukraine. Shevchenko's birthplace was also in the heart of Ukraine, in the centre on the Russian-ruled steppe. But Ivan Franko lived in sight of hardwood forests. He was born and raised not far from the Warwaruk village of Vovkhivsti. His Mykyta had places to hide. Places in the memory not forgotten during and after WWII:

His Foxburg is a famous fortress, crisscrossed with underground tunnels and provided with secret nooks and holes for hiding in.

During and after WWII, the enemies of Ukrainian Nationalists were Russians, Soviet Ukrainians, and Poles, not much different than Mykyta's enemies:

Lion, our Father (the Austrian Governor) *appointed Bear the Growler* (Russians) *to govern the entire highland forests.*

And the landlords were Polish. Fox Mykyta talks some more:

Exactly at that time Wolf the Hungry was determined to destroy me. Wolf and Bear volunteered to be the hangmen and promised to make fun of me as well. Where Bear rules, honour is trampled upon, freedom is lost, and truth is struck dumb.

And there were other animals: Billy Goat Basiliy, representing the scapegoat Jews. He is the Honourable Secretary of State, and there is Jack Yats the Rabbit, Chief of the Royal Guards.

Jump a century. During Ukraine's Maidan, US Assistant Secretary of State Victoria Nuland talked on the phone to Geoffrey Pyatt, the US Ambassador to Ukraine:

"...Yats is the guy..."

She's referring to Arseny Yatsenyuk, giving direction that he will be the future Prime Minister of Ukraine.

Ivan Franko's, *Jack Yats the Rabbit,* is Tsar Lev's *Chief of the Royal Guards.* In the fairytale *Fox Mykyta,* Yats and the goat talk about the social and political problems of the multicultural and multiracial empire.

Ukraine today?

And it may have been the same for Myhailo. During the war, because of his position, there'd be no escaping

To Find Myhailo

Vovkhivsti's social and political issues. Because he spoke German, Russian, Polish, and Ukrainian, he could talk to many people. His countryside's Tsar Lev was no longer *Fox Mykyta's* Austrian Governor. The new Tsar Lev was Joseph Stalin with his centralized politburo. He'd send his dictates to the distant Borschiv Soviet, and from there down through to Myhailo who'd bring the weekly orders to Vovkhivsti, along with sausage for his family. Myhailo was Vovkhivsti's Yats. He could provide favours, even for his own family.

To be Ukrainian or Polish had for centuries depended on which church a family attended - Ukrainian Catholic, or Roman Catholic. Vovkhivsti had both. At the time when Stalin was cleaning out Poles from Halychyna, in return for Ukrainians from western Poland, Myhailo changed his family's religion to Roman Catholic. This would increase his family's chances to get to Canada, to the place where Myhailo's Uncle Danylo had immigrated when Myhailo was a young boy. But he changed his mind. Myhailo soon reverted back to the Ukrainian Catholic Church. These dealings may have placed a black mark on his reputation in the eyes of Ukrainian Nationalists. In 1924, German/Jewish writer, Alfred Doblin noted in his travels through Halychyna:

They are very fond of German culture and Germany. But many Ukrainians disgorge a terrible, blind, numb hatred, an entirely animal hatred of the Poles.

When Stalin shipped Vovkhivsti's Polish families west to Poland, the villagers seized the opportunity to dismantle the Roman Catholic Church and use its building stones to build their barns.

The Ukraine of the war years, along with the Ukraine of today, have similarities to Ivan Franko's fairytale countryside. One result of the war was simply that a new *Tsar Lev* had *Bear the Growler* chase *Wolf the Hungry* back to

Poland. He cleansed western Ukraine of its Polish masters, only to put his bears in charge. Maidan has opened up a fight to rid Ukraine of bears, but what if the wolf comes back to claim his land? What scheme can Fox Mykyta now devise?

To Find Myhailo

CHAPTER 7

The places away
like the safety of fox dens
are the isolated villages of Ukraine
with gardens like my mother's were
with flowers from the seeds of her grandmother
brought on the boat
cloth pouches round her waist, filled with seeds.
Ukraine today with poppyseed and open wells.
Embroidery.
Church domes above the trees
the home of my forefathers.
I go once more to Vovkhivsti
to find Myhailo and Maria.
But not yet.
The winter has to pass.
We're hardly through Remembrance Day...
the baby-boomers dressed in tams
and navy blazers buttoned barely
over bellies, storefront soldiers selling poppies.
Raise the flag, sound the bugle,
but shield our eyes
from drones that do the killing...
Only fools and children tell the truth...
Not much has changed...
And as for children,
it was long ago...
I sit with English friends at
United Church Sunday School.
Glenavon has no domed Ukrainian church.
Stores are English-owned, but
Father bought one, and

Larry Warwaruk

Mother sells to wives of
Polish and Ukrainian farmers.
English women too.
Mother is skilled at telling people
what they want to hear,
inflecting Slav, or English,
talking cabbage rolls
or English plum pudding,
and in our Ukrainian-flowered yard
Mother's garden party
honours English dames austere
in bonnets laced with netted veils,
Mother serving tea and crumpets...
And now in my old age I meet a childhood friend
who tells me that back then in Glenavon
She didn't know I was Ukrainian...

To Find Myhailo

The dark side of my heritage runs deep.

In 1844 Nikolai Gogol wrote in a letter: *"I myself do not know whether my soul is Ukrainian or Russian. I know only that on no account would I give priority to the Little Russian before the Russian, or the Russian before the Little Russian"*.

David Lloyd George, Prime Minister of the United Kingdom, stated: *"I only saw a Ukrainian once. It is the last Ukrainian I have seen, and I am not sure I want to see any more."* In 1921 the delegates at the Treaty of Riga were confused about Ukrainians. They did not know whether the Greek Catholic Ruthenians from the Hapsburg Empire were the same people as the Orthodox Ukrainians from the Russian Empire. As written down in the Treaty of Riga, these Greek Catholic Ukrainians came under the rule of a newly formed Poland, and the Organization of Ukrainian Nationalists (OUN) soon formed to fight for an independent Ukraine. Throughout the 1920s and 30s the fight was against Polish domination. At a high school in the town of Berezhany, OUN members tore down a Polish flag and threw it into a toilet. A local Ukrainian who criticized this act was found dead shortly afterwards. In the same town, Polish high school students organized a *"funeral of Ukraine,"* marching through the town with a coffin marked *"Ukraine is dead."* After a few days, the bodies of two Poles who had taken part in the *"funeral"* were found in a nearby river.

Stepan Bandera joined the OUN in 1929. By the next year he was head of its propaganda section, and at its Berlin conference in June 1933, he became the leader of OUN's homeland executive. The following June, Poland's Minister of the Interior, Borislaw Pieracki, was assassinated. Bandera, who in the underground went by several aliases, one of them being *Lys (The Fox)* was hunted down and arrested as a chief instigator in the murder of Pieracki. On the 13th of January 1936, Bandera received the death penalty. However, less than two weeks before this, the Polish parliament had abolished capital punishment. His sentence was reduced to life imprisonment. When the verdict was announced, Bandera stood up, raised his right arm above his head, and called out, *"Slava Ukraini."*

This trial took place in Warsaw, and was followed up in Lviv with a second trial of twenty-three defendants. As Bandera entered the courtroom, he performed the fascist salute, raising his right arm slightly to the left and shouting again the famous call, *"Slava Ukraini!"*

Bandera was jailed in Brest until September 1939 when Nazi Germany invaded Poland. He escaped to Lviv but then realizing that Halychyna would be under Soviet rule, he made his way back to Nazi-ruled Poland where he worked to complete a document called *The Struggle and Activities of the OUN in Wartime:*

 -*Death to Muscovite-Jewish communism!*
 -*Marxism - a Jewish creation!*
 -*Kill the Enemies among You, the Jews and Informers!*
 -*It is Better to Destroy National Property than to Give it to the Muscovite Stealers!*
 -*Ukrainian Property into Ukrainian Hands!*

On the 22nd of June, 1941, Nazi Germany invaded the Soviet Union. Ten days later German troops entered the Ukrainian city of Ternopil. Triumphal arches displayed German and Ukrainian flags. Banners proclaimed *"Glory to Ukraine - Glory to Bandera!" "Long Live the German Army!" "Long Live the Leader of the German Nation Adolf Hitler!" "Freedom for Ukraine - Death to Moscow!" "Glory to our Leader Stepan Bandera!"*

To Find Myhailo

This was Myhailo's time, a crucial time where his need was great to tell his superiors what they wanted to hear. Bandera Ukrainians would have told the Germans that Myhailo had been a member of the Borschiv Soviet, yet through the three years of German rule he remained as Mayor of Vovkhivsti. Bandera Ukrainians showed no mercy to Soviet collaborators: in the Lviv region in August 1944, OUN/UPA members gouged out the eyes of members of two whole families, one by one in front of the others, and then hacked them to pieces in front of the villagers.

My heritage? Or is it better to flush such memory away? Change the history? In 1957, a book appeared in the Diaspora: *I Am alive Thanks to the UPA*, a short autobiography of Stella Krentsbakh, compiled by Petro Mirchuk and V. Davydenko. Before the War, Petro Mirchuk headed a propaganda division for the Organization of Ukrainian Nationalists (OUN). After the War he was in DP camps until 1950, when he then settled in the United States to spend much of his time writing publications for the glory and honour of OUN and UPA.

Mirchuk wrote the story of Stella Krentsbakh. He wrote that the woman was born in Bolekhiv in the Lviv region. That she was the daughter of a rabbi, graduating from Lviv University to then serve as a nurse and intelligence agent with UPA. He wrote that in the spring of 1945 the NKVD captured her. That she was imprisoned, tortured, and sentenced to death. But UPA soldiers managed to free her and she escaped into the Carpathian Mountains to finally reach the British Zone in Austria. Eventually she reached Israel. She wrote: *"I attribute the fact that I am alive today and devoting all the strength of my thirty-eight years to a free Israel, only to God and the Ukrainian Insurgent Army."*

Larry Warwaruk

There is only one problem with the story: Stella Krentsbakh was a fabrication - a slick attempt to paint over any suggestion that Bandera's soldiers might have harmed innocent Jews.

Reading about the devious ploys and subterfuge of Bandera and OUN/UPA stresses me with negative thoughts about Ukrainians. How should I read the following words of Otto Von Bismarck - his viewpoint of Ukrainians who existed in the time prior to my grandparents' emigration. Bismarck played a leading role in the 1870s unification of Germany. I have no idea if his opinion of Ukrainians was his alone, or whether it represented the views of other Germans. The people he describes would have been a part of my people. They were surely not as bad as an arrogant German of a self-defined *Master Race* might determine. Yet still, they give me pause to reflect on my origins as I'm again reminded of the horrific female image depicted on the 3rd floor of the Odessa Union Hall:

Someone had garroted her with a wire. She's bent over backwards against a desk, her protruding belly pointed at the ceiling, her head fastened down to the desktop...

This was an act that would fit into Bismarck's Prussian upper class opinion of the Ukrainian peasantry in Austrian-ruled Halychyna:

"There is nothing more vile and disgusting than the so-called 'Ukrainians.' This rabble, nurtured by the Poles from the most vile scum of the Russian people - murderers, careerists, creepy before intelligentsia, ready for power and profitable place to kill their own fathers and mothers! These bastards are willing to break their own countrymen, not even for profit, but to satisfy their baser instincts. For them nothing is sacred, betrayal is the norm, they are mis-

To Find Myhailo

erable of mind, spiteful, jealous, cunning, and especially tricky. These subhumans absorbed all the worst and basest qualities of the soul from the Russians, Poles, and Austrians, leaving the good qualities untouched. Most of all, they hate their benefactors, those who have done good to them, and they are always ready to grovel before the mighty of the world. They are fit for nothing and can perform only primitive work. They will never be able to create their own state. Many countries drove them like a ball throughout Europe, and slavish instincts are so engrained in them that all their essence is covered with loathsome sores."

Certainly not all Ukrainians. It must be most certainly only a very few like the Odessa Union Hall perpetrators.

Yet, in the history of my heritage, there is a more general aspect of a dark side. In 1898, a Ukrainian priest from Pennsylvania wrote the following about migrants in the Dauphin area. My people. Those from Vovkhivsti who came from the Borschiv area in Ukraine. They homesteaded in Volga, north of Dauphin, not that far east of the area the priest mentions:

"I came across several of our people here, mainly from the Borschow area, (Polish spelling) who bring only disgrace upon our nation. Although some of them have been here several months, they still appear dirty and look wretched, and they still wear their old-country clothes and their hair long. In no way can they be persuaded to switch fashions. If they did, they say, they would lose their faith. One wife threatened to drown or hang herself if her husband dared to get his hair cut.

And on the floor in the Dauphin immigration hostel:

"Right in the middle of the floor is our muzhik making himself at home as he repeatedly prostrates himself, forehead to the floor, till the room resounds with thuds...."

I'm troubled more and more with the writing of this story - not so much concerning Myhailo and Maria, but I'm deeply worried about where to go with what's happening - atrocities like the Odessa Union Hall. Am I traitor to my ethnicity? A decade ago I began to treasure the symbols of Ukraine. I'd wear embroidered shirts. I have a cloth of patterned weave my great-grandmother in 1903 brought with her from Vovkhivsti - my mother's heirloom handed down. But now the blue and yellow flags, the black and red, give me the chills. I had been searching for my essence, but today's parades are not those of my forefathers.

Yet I must go once more to Vovkhivsti,

CHAPTER 8

The week in early June, 2016

I had contacted Anatole by email that we were planning another trip to Ukraine. He replied that he'd be more than happy once again to be our guide. But then for the longest while I heard nothing, and I wondered if he'd been called to the war, or if he'd gone into hiding which I thought better suited Anatole.

I emailed Natalya in Lviv to see if she could contact him. The phone number I had for Anatole was no longer in service which made me think that he and his family had fled to Romania. Natalya wasn't able to locate him, but just days before our flight was to leave, I finally got an email. Anatole was waiting for us, assuring us that he would guarantee a safe and comfortable time in Ukraine. He sent another phone number for us to make the final arrangements. He would drive the eight hours up from Chernivsti to get us in Lviv.

It's Sunday afternoon and tourists fill Lviv's market square. Street posters display scenes of Donbas carnage. One shows the photographs of the *Heavenly Hundred,* some of whom snipers on a rooftop gunned down at Maidan. Half a dozen or so young men in army fatigues stroll about the square. The general mood of the afternoon is not of war. A few black and red Bandera flags flutter, and many more of Ukraine's blue and yellow. But somehow the patriotic colours are faded, as if tired. Yet there are reminders. On a souvenir table I see a roll of toilet paper with Putin's face inked on every square.

Natalya's father is a seismic engineer who had worked several years for a Russian oil company. He had just got back from an eight month stint in Siberia. He doesn't want to work for the Russians any more but he and Natalya are going to Kyiv to arrange for his pension from the compa-

To Find Myhailo

ny. He wants to pay four year's university tuition for his son so that he can be exempt from a call up.

When Anatole arrives I find out why we hadn't heard from him. He'd been called up three times to train recruits. His camp held two hundred men along with Nato trainers from Britain, Canada, and the USA. These officers had special camp facilities for themselves. Anatole had cold water showers and buckwheat porridge. Most of what he did with his trainees was to scrape the rust off antiquated weapons that had been in longtime storage. The only way for him to be paid was to sign a contract that he'd go to fight in the Donbas. He refused. Many who had gone did not receive their money, and if they were maimed or killed, their families were not provided for. Anatole says that if he had got another call that happened to interfere with the time of our visit, he had arranged with his wife's brother (who is a surgeon) that if needed, he'd put a cast on Anatole's wrist and write up a medical exemption. But still, the Russians are the enemy. Anatole is waiting to enroll his four year-old son Andriy into the Ivan Bohun Military School in Kyiv. They take boys starting at the age of ten. The boy Andriy will train to have a life-long career that pays real money.

The tree-lined highway heads south from Lviv. The Soviet-era asphalt crumbles around potholes, but shiny new Opels and Mercedes cars zip around them at high speed. The landmarks have changed from the granite monoliths of Red Army soldiers, to modern gas stations - Chevron, Shell, OKO - the beacons of the new wished-for Ukraine. The Soviet monuments are all gone now, totally replaced by the many flowered Bandera mohylas - (earthen mounds). On a hillside a WW2 Red Army tank has been painted yellow and blue - colours fading in the sun. And it seems through every village, the black and red, and yellow and blue painted gates and fences are starting to fade. But the new gas stations sparkle as signs of the coming western future.

Yet there are times where the past can be celebrated. Ten weeks after Easter in Vovkhivsti, thousands come to the church to have their very biggest sins forgiven. They parade around the church with a replica of a holy icon. Five hundred and seventy-five years ago monks came from afar with an icon of the Virgin Mary. They built a church and the village was born.

A young priest shows us the icon where it hangs on the wall at the back of the sanctuary. Never is it removed and never is it shown to the public. And here I am, from far away, returned. Oddly, I feel the icon's aura. In this secluded place, I gaze upward to this golden symbol of my deepest roots. Would my great-grandparents, before they came to Canada, have paraded around this church with a replica of this icon?

In 1807 a Polish landlord demanded that it be placed in the village's Roman Catholic Church. His servant's hands froze to the icon when he reached to take it down. The landlord realized its miraculous powers. Only after he promised that the icon would remain in the Ukrainian Catholic Church, did the servant's hands release. The landlord had the icon restored, and had it gilded with the finest gold. The priest knows of three occasions where women, who had been unable to conceive, had a priest pray to it for thirty days. The women conceived.

Our first trip to the village was in 2007 where in the afternoon we met Tetiana and her mother. Olya translated that they had come to join the celebrations at the church for the 200th anniversary of the sighting of the Virgin Mary. It's just now that I learn the real story. Every year on the 10th Sunday after Easter, thousands of people come from

To Find Myhailo

all around to celebrate the miraculous powers of the golden icon. Our first visit to the village was two hundred years after the hands of the servant froze fast to the icon.

I learn more details of Myhailo's abduction. His grandson, Bohdan, comes to have dinner with us at the Shatoshok Hotel. I ask him about the story where in 1967 bones were found in a well and people thought they were Myhailo's.

"Never heard of such a thing," Bohdan says. In 1967 Bohdan would have been in his teens. Surely if bones had been found, and if his parents had been discussing funeral arrangements, he would remember. He also said that he'd never heard anything about Myhailo having been dragged behind a horse. He said that in 1945 it would have been highly unlikely for UPA insurgents to put on such a display. With the Germans gone, UPA was in hiding. It's likely that a band simply shot Myhailo, or it could have thrown him down a well.

As for the abduction, the Soviets had issued an amnesty. If an insurgent surrendered his weapons, he would be pardoned.

"Late one night," Bohdan says, "two men on horses came to Myhailo's house. My father and his younger brother Vasyl were staying with their aunt. The oldest brother Ivan was listening from the attic."

The two men gave their guns to Myhailo, and he gave them documents that granted them amnesty. Two nights later while Myhailo still had the guns in the house, another two men came on horses. They said they were from the NKVD and that they had come to collect the guns. Myhailo was ordered to come with them as some of his papers had to be corrected. I recall what Vasyl and Maria had told me about his judges - the three women and two men who held his trial through that night and the following day. The two men who took him that night were from UPA.

Myhailo was never seen again.

Besides Bohdan, we talk with village elders. How did the people regard Myhailo?

In those years people kept their thoughts to themselves. Nobody wanted jobs like Myhailo's. Nobody wanted to be a school teacher. Most of these positions were filled by outsiders. When the Soviets came in the spring of 1940, the livestock and equipment from the Polish farm disappeared overnight. It was Myhailo's responsibility to get these belongings returned to the people's new collective. The hunt went overboard, scavenging even the foundation stones of people's houses. The same thing happened in 1991 when the collectives were dismantled. The belongings disappeared overnight.

Some of the villagers were for Myhailo. Some against. The elders tell me that Myhailo asked that the UPA soldiers he had billeted over the 1944 Christmas Season remember his good deeds. Maybe they did, but to no avail. Half a year later he was taken.

Villagers either sided with UPA, or they worked for the collective. Do families after all these years hold any grudges? The elders didn't think so. This was so long into the past. They remember that the Soviet authorities had been on the hunt of a local UPA activist for twenty-five years. After all that time they finally caught him. He was brought before the villagers who said to leave him be. What good to punish an old man for deeds that were best forgotten? Let bygones be bygones.

The Dudka family claims that Symon was not responsible for Myhailo's abduction. Bohdan doesn't agree. Symon

To Find Myhailo

Dudka being the head of a local UPA band, it's highly likely that he would have known what was to take place. Would he have known the names of the two men and three women who judged Myhailo? The trial took place in a village house throughout the remainder of the night and all through the following day. Vasyl and Maria Warwaruk told me these names. Vasyl's mother had told Vasyl and his brothers. No one was to know, but it wasn't long before the village knew. But no one would tell.

What about the fifteen Jewish families from Vovkhivsti who were rounded up and taken to the Ghetto in Borschiv, where on the outskirts they were shot and buried? What I hear from the village elders is that these families would have fled beforehand, and other Jews from Borschiv would have come to the village to hide. A Solomon woman had been a house-keeper for Sosia Flintenstein in Borschiv, and she then hid the Jewish woman and her son in the kerosene storage caves under the Solomon house. Myhailo's wife and mother helped out with provisions of bread and cheese.

Maria Horbova who was hanged? I learn this time that it was her younger sister who was somewhat simple. Maria was quite intelligent. The elders tell me that it was old women spreading nasty rumors that got Maria Horbova hanged. I think of her at age 19, and myself. This age for me was a time to look ahead. For her it was a time to hang from a rope tied to a tree beside the hall. It was a time of death, with a last glimpse down to a pool of healing waters of a flowing stream, where on Pentecost, villagers bathe. In that 1949 Soviet time did the old ladies bathe their feet in these waters?

Today this place still has the over-hanging trees, and the remains of the old hall's stone-work foundation. Below these broken stones, new stone-work walls enclose the healing waters. The old steps that led up to the hall now lead to a plain white chapel and storeroom, potted flowers along the top step at the doorway. By all appearances, this location of Maria's death is now a place of holiness, as it likely was back then.

To Find Myhailo

October, 2016

Many of the villages in Halychyna, if not all of them, have a Soviet-erected Red Army monument for its fallen heroes, a monument contrasted to another that honours those that fought against them, as if each village had its own civil war. Vovkhivsti has its *monument to the fighters for the freedom of Ukraine,* with its list of names, and it has its *Great Patriotic War* monument with the names of Myhailo and Maria, and many others, followed with the inscription Glory to the Victorious People. Nowhere in the village does it says that the heroes on these two monuments fought against each other. I've just noticed on *Facebook* that someone has posted pictures of the two monuments in the village of Sapohiv that is just a few kilometres to the south of Vovkhivsti. It has its *monument to the fighters for the freedom of Ukraine,* and the other is called *monument to the fallen in WWII.* No mention is made to what used to be *The Great Patriotic War,* and the inscription *Glory to the Victorious People* has been erased. I'm curious to know if the same has been done in Vovkhivsti.

  I've hired a law firm from Lviv to search the archives for information on the life and death of Myhailo. So far they've found nothing other than his father Teodor's birth, and that of his brother Maksym. In a book, *Chronicle of UPA,* mention is made about Myhailo being a village administrator. Nothing is said about his death. They've found that in 1946 his brother Maksym was appointed to the executive committee of Vovkhivsti's village council. I find it strange that there is information about Maksym, yet nothing on Myhailo. Has he been removed from the Soviet archives in the current government's attempt to rewrite Ukraine's history?

  No mention is made of Maria. Erased like the *Glory to the Victorious People* inscription?

To Find Myhailo

As I wait for more information, I scan through a book I had found in my late father's belongings: *The Basis of Durable Peace,* published in 1917: articles written by an American writer, Cosmos, in the New York Times. One of the articles refers to Russia and the Slavs:

-The Latin, the Anglo-Saxon, and the Teuton have made their distinctive contributions to our common civilization...

-The Slav, however, has yet to make his full contribution to the general store of the world's intellectual and political capital...

Of particular note for me is that nowhere in the chapter is mention made of Ukrainians. Reference is made to Poles fortunate enough to live under the civilizing tendencies of the Germanic Hapsburg Empire, as opposed to those having to live further east under the Russians. In this New York Times' book published in January 1917, it appears that there was no general knowledge of Ukrainians. They were either Poles or Russians. As referred to earlier in this story, British Prime Minister, Lloyd George, encountered Ukrainian Nationalists:

"I only saw a Ukrainian once. It is the last Ukrainian I have seen, and I am not sure I want to see any more."

In 1921 the delegates at the Treaty of Riga were confused about Ukrainians. They did not know whether the Greek Catholic Ruthenians from the Hapsburg Empire were the same people as the Orthodox Ukrainians from the Russian Empire. By this time in Canada my great-grandfather Danylo was saving up money to build a cultural hall in Vovkhivsti.- the very hall beside which Maria Horbova was hanged.

Seven decades later on the third floor of the Odessa Union Hall, the garroted young woman is seated on the edge of a desk, the back of her head pinned down to the desktop. Does anyone care? Does anyone in Canada or the United States even know about the Odessa Union Hall massacre? And if the people did, would they care?

Just blame Putin.

Fox Mykyta performs for the Ukrainian Canadian Congress. Its Uke Tube videos display Mykyta's skills through interviews by authors of books that blame all of Ukraine's misfortunes on Putin and the Russians. Writer James Kirchick says that the first narrative the Russians put forth on the Maidan was that Ukrainians were fascists, Nazis and right wing extremists. That narrative did not work. The new narrative is that Ukraine is a hopelessly corrupt and broken state. Supporting Ukraine is a waste of money that will be stolen.

To fight Russian propaganda and Russia's information war against Ukraine, we (the west, Ukraine) should not sink to their level and disseminate lies and propaganda.
Ethnic conflict in Ukraine was fiction. It was completely made up by Russia.

No Nazis in Ukraine? I think of the Odessa Union Hall Massacre. And of Myhailo dragged behind a horse.

To Find Myhailo

*In searching for Myhailo
I found three sons, and
his house that was his father's
and that of his father's father,
the same house that bore
my great grandfather, Danylo.
And up the hill I saw the church
in back of which
the icon hangs
of near six hundred years.
And before the cemetery
countless puffs of dandelions
gone to seed.
Into the hardwood forest,
Myhailo's trail.
It's here I find myself?
My Ukrainian self,
Back in time?
Back to the muzyk' s forehead
that pounds upon the floor?
Back to Danylo's culture hall -'prosvita'
'to the light?'
And to my mother's side
her father fled the tsar's empire
to freedom in Halychyna
to change his name to 'Freedom,'
in Russian, 'Sloboda.'
Ukrainian, 'Svoboda.'
'Slobodzian' was my mother's maiden name.
My father, a young man in 1930
a student in the first graduation class
of the Dauphin Normal School.
My Ukrainian-speaking father*

Larry Warwaruk

schooled to teach English
to Ukrainian-speaking children.
Years later in my childhood
everything was English.
No Ukrainian for me.
On the street was English.
And though my father's generation
did have some firm beliefs
of who they were, they did not have
the war-steeped blood-lust drive
of post-1945 emigres.
Disciples of Bandera
Red and black the flag
Grandsons of these disciples
Ukrainian Canadian Congress
Canada's new Ukrainian voice
that has the government's ear
the call for cash and guns and men
to fight the Putin Russians in Donbass.
To help the Fox Mykytas fight the bear.

...

Nov. 8 email from Anatole:
"Two more times Military Commission
calls me -
but I ignore them.
Ukraine has young people to go fight.
I have had enough military adventures."

To Find Myhailo

November 11, 2016 Remembrance Day...
I get my latest information from the Lviv law firm. The Borschiv police have no record of the Warwaruk family because Vovkhivsti records go back only so far as 1950.
Yet from the State archive of the Ternopil region: *Within the protocol (record) of meeting No. 10 of 16.5 1946 of the executive committee of Borschiv regional council there is data of appointment of Mr. Warwaruk Maksym* (Myhailo's brother) *as a member of executive committee of Vovkhivti village council.*
Myhailo Warwaruk was taken in 1945. Maria Horbova was hanged in 1949. No record...
In 1946 Maksym Warwaruk was appointed to the very village council from which Myhailo was forcibly removed never to be seen again. Record exists of one brother. Not the other.
The Ukrainian Patriotic Army in the Borschiv area kept some records. They show that in 1945 its units executed two communists, three komsomols, two functionaries, one collective farm manager, six informers, twelve active supporters of the Soviets, and two village heads. Their names are not listed. Not Maria Horbova's. Not Myhailo's. He was one of the two village heads. All of these, Soviet no-names. Three days after Christmas the Lviv law firm inform me that Ukraine's State Archives have nothing about the deaths of Myhailo and Maria. I ask whether it's possible that the information has been removed. They say that it's possible that the Soviets took the files back to Russia after the fall of the Soviet Union. I ask whether the information could have been removed as a result of the current government's decommunization laws. Get rid of everything that might make the history of the Bandera Movement look bad.

The circumstances surrounding the deaths of Myhailo and Maria would certainly do that.

In 1946 Maksym Warwaruk was appointed to the very village council from which his brother was forcibly removed never to be seen again. There's nothing on Myhailo. Nothing about Myhailo being dragged behind a horse. Nothing on Maria Horbova being hanged in the winter, barefoot from a tree.

No answer from the law firm.

Only fools and children tell the truth.

www.ingramcontent.com/pod-product-compliance
Lightning Source LLC
Chambersburg PA
CBHW070044120526
44589CB00035B/2305